D1359729

Beyond Reagan

Setting the Next Agenda

Timely Reports to Keep
Journalists, Scholars and the Public
Abreast of Developing Issues, Events and Trends

WITHDRAWN

Editorial Research Reports
Published by Congressional Quarterly Inc.
1414 22nd Street, N.W.
Washington, D.C. 20037

371333

Tennessee Tech. Library
Cookeville, Tenn.

About the Cover

The cover was designed by Staff Artist Robert Redding

Copyright 1987 by Congressional Quarterly Inc.
publisher of Editorial Research Reports

The right to make direct commercial use of material in Editorial Research Reports is strictly reserved to magazine, newspaper, radio and television clients of the service.

PRINTED IN THE UNITED STATES OF AMERICA

Editor, Hoyt Gimlin
Assistant, Susan Waterman
Production Manager, I. D. Fuller
Assistant Production Manager, Maceo Mayo

Library of Congress Cataloging-in-Publication Data

Beyond Reagan.

Ten reports originally published as separate issues of Editorial research reports.
Bibliography: p.
Includes index.
Contents: America's service economy — Working on welfare — Home care — [etc.]
1. United States — Economic policy — 1981-1987.
2. United States — Social policy.   I. Congressional Quarterly, inc.   II. Editorial research reports.
HC106.8.B47   1987   338.973   87-3057
ISBN 0-87187-437-7

Contents

Foreword

The basic outlook of America and its president generally must coincide if he is to achieve success in office and this country a sense of purpose. Opinion polls and many other shreds of evidence tell us that a majority of the American people were receptive to Ronald Reagan's advice and began to feel better about themselves and their country as he entered the White House. They were eager to move beyond the doubts and misgivings of the Vietnam era and into the American morning he portrayed. His vision prevailed over scoffers and skeptics, winning the day repeatedly in the legislative arena. He was able to enlist the electorate's backing for his broader aims of lowering taxes, shrinking the federal role at home, and asserting the U.S. role abroad.

Now the pundits and pollsters say the public's mood is shifting, that the nation is moving into a "post-Reagan era." As expressed this spring by *Time* essayist Lance Morrow, "There are signs of fundamental change in the nation's political weather, a philosophical mood shift like those that seem to occur in America every generation or so."

Even before the Iran-contra affair arose, sapping Reagan's presidential strength, there was talk of a new national agenda being formed to emphasize unmet social needs. A break with what has preceded is not uncommon — indeed almost customary — during the final two years of a presidency. It is especially likely to occur if the president's party suffered defeat in the mid-term election, as Reagan's did last November. The field of 1988 presidential candidates already is becoming crowded, and each is portraying his own vision of national affairs.

Other than on the hustings, where are the signs of fundamental change, of which Morrow and others now write? One is in the polling by the firm of Yankelovich Clancy Shulman for Morrow's magazine, which reported that by February 77 percent of the people surveyed said the federal government should take a more active role in such areas as health, housing, education and help for the poor. Only 31 percent still supported increased spending for military purposes, and 61 percent disapproved of cutbacks in social programs.

As reported elsewhere, the Gallup Organization has detected a greater public interest in foreign affairs since 1982. However, it has been pointed out that much of this interest is self-interest, especially in the desire of Americans to protect their jobs from foreign competition. Three of the ten reports in this book — on industrial competitiveness, dollar diplomacy and America's service economy — look at how different aspects of fierce competition from abroad affect the livelihood of Americans, and will continue to affect them.

No agenda can ignore the basic war-and-peace issues, of which arms control has long been central in U.S.-Soviet relations. One of the reports examines the lively prospect that the two superpowers and their European allies may come to terms on reducing, even eliminating, nuclear missiles on that continent. Beyond lies the dizzying but no longer unthinkable possibility of nuclear disarmament virtually worldwide, such as Reagan and his Soviet counterpart, Mikhail S. Gorbachev, so tentatively and tantalizingly discussed at their Iceland summit meeting.

Among the big social issues that will doubtlessly move into the post-Reagan era are those addressed in this book's reports on home and catastrophic health care for the elderly, national policy affecting the family, and the developing trend that ties welfare to work. Another report, on fresh calls for non-military national service for America's youth, indicates a reawakened spirit of liberal idealism in the late 1980s. Those calls suggest a national dissatisfaction with "Me Generation" attitudes and strike echoes from President Kennedy's admonition, "Ask not what your country can do for you...."

Two other reports round out this book. One examines the Rehnquist Court, which may well become the Reagan administration's most enduring legacy, although as yet the court's rightward tilt has been less than was expected. Finally, there is a look at how the arid West is coming to terms with its scarcity of water. Some leaders have suggested that water may be the "sleeper" issue that will command far greater attention in the years ahead. We think that together the 10 reports address a sizable share of national concerns to be sorted through in the agenda-setting process for the post-Reagan years.

Hoyt Gimlin
Editor

May 1987
Washington, D.C.

v

AMERICA'S SERVICE ECONOMY

by

Mary H. Cooper

June 27
1 9 8 6

Service Sector Growth

As America heads into its fourth year of recovery from the worst recession since the 1930s, there is much good news for consumers. Several trends have brought about an emerging consensus among economists that economic conditions are better than they have been for a decade or more and that they can be expected to continue at least through 1987. The oil price decline brought about a fall in the consumer price index to 3.8 percent last year, the lowest level since 1967. Interest rates have also slid, reducing the cost of credit and bringing home ownership once again within the reach of many Americans. The fall in interest rates also promises to make the dollar less attractive to overseas investors, easing the upward pressure on the currency's exchange value. The weaker dollar — which has depreciated by 27 percent from its peak value in February 1985 — makes U.S. products less expensive to foreign consumers and thus should improve their competitiveness on world markets.

But there is a dark side to the recovery. It has passed by large parts of the country where oil and farming are prominent.[1] Civilian unemployment, at 7.3 percent, remains at its highest level ever so far into a recovery. America's trade balance, for all the encouraging news on the dollar, registered a $148.5 billion deficit in 1985 and is not expected this year to improve much, if at all. For the first time since World War I, the value of foreign assets in the United States has since mid-1985 exceeded that of U.S. assets abroad, bringing the country the dubious honor of having nudged out Brazil as the world's biggest debtor nation.

To explain these contradictions, economists point increasingly to a fundamental shift in the American economy away from the manufacture of goods to the provision of services. Some observers place the emergence of a service-based economy on a par with the industrial revolution, which by World War I had transferred the bulk of American labor from the farms to the factories. The United States, free of warfare at home and significant competition from abroad, emerged as the world's leading industrial power. Its economic well-being depended on the basic goods-producing industries — mining, construction and manufacturing — in addition to agriculture.

---

[1] For background on these two troubled sectors of the economy, see "Oil Prices: Collapse and Consequences," *E.R.R.*, 1986 Vol. I, pp. 249-264; and "Farm Finance: Deepening Debt Crisis," *E.R.R.*, 1986 Vol. I, pp. 265-288.

Services grew as a natural corollary to basic industry. In fact, if services are defined in their broadest sense *(see next page)*, more Americans have been engaged in producing services than goods at least since 1919, when the Labor Department began recording employment trends. But the growing role of the service sector did not become fully apparent until the early 1980s, when it was virtually the only source of new jobs in the United States. Although Western Europe and Japan had steadily eroded America's dominance of the world market in manufactured goods since the end of World War II, it was not until the late 1970s that these inroads were felt in terms of widespread layoffs in such basic U.S. industries as automobiles and steel.

The recession of 1981-82 compounded the goods-producing sector's difficulties, as factory orders plummeted. Unemployment reached its highest levels since the 1930s Depression; almost three million production workers in manufacturing, mining and construction lost their jobs. Some one million of these, who had been laid off temporarily during previous downturns, found their work places closed for good. Industries left in apparently permanent decline include steelmaking, textiles and shoe manufacturing — all unable to compete with foreign imports despite large wage concessions gained from their workers in recent years. President Reagan's military buildup has kept jobs in some defense-related industries, and workers have flocked to such high-technology fields as robot and computer making. But they have not been strong enough to offset the loss of jobs elsewhere. The energy sector, which had enjoyed a boom in the wake of oil price increases during the 1970s, stagnated in the 1980s and now is in the grips of a depression.

Export of Services; Theories Behind Growth

Virtually unscathed by the turmoil in manufacturing and mining, the service economy continues to expand. According to a government report, the share of jobs in services rose steadily from 62 to 72 percent of all non-agricultural employment between 1960 and 1980. Over the same period, some 86 percent of all new jobs were in the service economy.[2] The trend has continued: fully 75 percent of the non-farm jobs in the first quarter of 1986 were in services, and only 25 percent in the production of goods.

As the service economy has expanded, so has U.S. dependence on the export of services to other nations. While more difficult to monitor than trade in goods, the International Trade Administration in the U.S. Commerce Department estimates that service exports, including investment income, rose from $132

---

[2] Office of the U.S. Trade Representative, "U.S. National Study on Trade in Services: A Submission by the United States Government to the General Agreement on Tariffs and Trade," 1984.

Defining the Service Economy

The common point of reference among all government agencies in their tracking of business trends is the Standard Industrial Classification (SIC) System, a listing administered by the Office of Management and Budget. By SIC's broadest definition of the service economy, it excludes only industries involved in the production of goods: construction, manufacturing and mining. The service economy thus includes the three levels of government — federal, state and local — and the following five broad categories of private industry:

1. *Transportation and public utilities* (incl. communications)
2. *Wholesale trade* (durable and non-durable goods)
3. *Retail trade*
   — Building materials and garden supplies
   — General merchandise stores
   — Food stores
   — Automotive dealers and service stations
   — Apparel and accessory stores
   — Furniture and home furnishings stores
   — Eating and drinking places
   — Miscellaneous retail
4. *Finance, insurance and real estate*
5. *Services*
   — Hotels and other lodging places
   — Personal services
   — Business services
   — Auto repair, services and garages
   — Miscellaneous repair services
   — Motion pictures
   — Amusement and recreation services
   — Health services
   — Legal services
   — Educational services
   — Social services
   — Museums, botanical and zoological gardens
   — Membership organizations
   — Miscellaneous services

billion in 1983 to more than $142 billion in 1984. To date, the United States has enjoyed surpluses in its trade in services with the rest of the world, thus reducing the growing deficit in merchandise trade.

The shift toward a service-based economy is attributed to many factors. Technological advances, especially in computers and telecommunications, have increased the dependence of goods-producing industries on such services as data processing. As automation of the assembly line has eliminated blue-collar positions, a growing number of jobs within goods-producing industries have been in such service areas as advertising and accounting. At the same time, there has been a trend among manufacturers to contract with outside firms to provide services from cleaning to computer maintenance. As more women have entered the labor market, day-care centers and restaurants have taken over some of the services previously provided by home-makers. Nursing homes and other health-care facilities have expanded as the population has grown older.

Audrey Freedman of the Conference Board, a New York-based business research organization, sees a structural cause for the shift to a service economy, and finds it typical of all indus-trial economies. As technology reduces the amount of direct labor required to produce goods, workers are "pushed forward" in the production sequence, ever closer to the point of contact with the final user.

Freedman cites the production of cotton bandages as an example. Because of automated equipment in the field and factory, relatively little labor is now required to produce the cotton and the packaged bandage. But once the bandage reaches the hospital, workers must store it and later take it to the proper ward. There, highly skilled labor is needed, as doc-tors and nurses work at the final point of the goods-production sequence by applying the bandage to the final user, the patient. Freeman writes that it is mostly service industries that are engaged in the final steps of providing goods. What most of them have in common is their detachment from the production process itself.[3]

Job Expansion in the 'Hamburger Economy'

The fastest-growing parts of the service sector have been some of the "service industries" themselves. They accounted for more than 22 million jobs by January 1986, according to the Bureau of Labor Statistics.[4] Of these, the largest number of jobs — more than six million — were found in the health services, including those in doctors' and dentists' offices, nursing homes, hospitals, laboratories and outpatient care facilities. Business services, with more than 4.5 million workers, rank second in service-sector employment and are expected to create the most new jobs in the next few years *(See p. 13.)*

This growth is attributed partly to the tendency of businesses to contract out for services they once provided with their in-house staffs. These services include advertising; consumer credit reporting and collection; mailing, copying and stenography; building maintenance; personnel; computer and data process-ing; research and development, management and consulting,

---

[3] Audrey Freedman, "Perspectives on Employment," Conference Board, May 5, 1986, p. 14.
[4] U.S. Department of Labor, Bureau of Labor Statistics, "Employment & Earnings," March 1986.

Fastest Growing . . .

. . . Industries	Average annual rate of change 1984-95
Medical services	4.3%
Business services	4.2
Computers and peripheral equipment	3.7
Materials handling equipment	3.7
Transportation services	3.5
Professional services	3.5
Scientific and controlling instruments	2.9
Medical instruments and supplies	2.8
Doctors' and dentists' services	2.6
Plastics products	2.5

. . . Occupations

Paralegal personnel	97.5%
Computer programmers	71.7
Computer systems analysts, electronic data processing (EDP)	68.7
Medical assistants	62.0
Data processing equipment repairers	56.2
Electrical and electronics engineers	52.8
Electrical and electronics technicians and technologists	50.7
Computer operators, except peripheral equipment	46.1
Peripheral EDP equipment operators	45.0
Travel agents	43.9

Fastest Declining . . .

. . . Industries	Average annual rate of change 1984-95
Cotton	−4.2%
Wooden Containers	−3.6
Leather products including footwear	−2.8
Iron and ferroalloy ores mining	−2.7
Sugar	−2.7
Leather tanning and finishing	−2.6
Railroad transportation	−2.6
Nonferrous metal ores mining, except copper	−2.6
Dairy products	−2.3
Blast furnaces and basic steel products	−2.2

. . . Occupations

Stenographers	−40.3%
Shoe sewing machine operators and tenders	−31.5
Railroad brake, signal, and switch operators	−26.4
Rail car repairers	−22.3
Furnace, kiln, or kettle operators and tenders	−20.9
Shoe and leather workers and repairers, precision	−18.6
Private household workers	−18.3
Station installers and repairers, telephone	−17.4
Sewing machine operators, garment	−16.7
Textile machine operators, tenders, setters, and set-up operators, winding	−15.7

Source: Projections by Bureau of Labor Statistics

and protective services. Of all the business services, those involving computer work and data processing have grown the fastest, by 250 percent in 1974-84. Within this field, demand has been especially strong for computer-programming services.[5]

The trade segment of the service economy is the biggest employer of all, and it has probably attracted the most attention — as the "hamburger economy," the derisive term used by workers displaced from goods-producing industries who fear they will end up flipping hamburgers in fast-food outlets. Employment in wholesale and retail trade stood at 5.8 million and 17.6 million. Eating and drinking places accounted for the largest number of jobs (5.5 million), followed by food stores (2.9 million) and general merchandise stores (2.4 million), including department and variety stores.

Jobs also increased in finance, insurance and real estate, which together employed six million workers in January. Much of the growth is traced to increases in productivity that result from advances in computers and communications. Although computers have wiped out many jobs involved with paperwork, they have enabled banking, insurance and real estate to expand customer services, thus boosting employment overall.

Growth has been slower in the other main segments of the service economy: (1) transportation and public utilities, and (2) government. Transportation and utilities employ about five million people in broadcasting and telephone communications, shipping and passenger transportation, and in gas and electric companies. Deregulation of airlines, trucking, railroads and the telephone system, combined with the breakup of the American Telephone & Telegraph Co. (AT&T), caused widespread employment shifts but little job growth overall. Government jobs at the federal, state and local levels have also remained fairly stable, accounting for 16.5 million this year.

Many of the trends in service employment are expected to continue for the foreseeable future *(See graph, p. 11.)* Of the 16 million new jobs the Bureau of Labor Statistics projects will be added to the economy by 1995, nine out of 10 will be in the service economy. Business, personal and medical services are expected to account for almost half of the new jobs and one-quarter of all jobs in the U.S. economy. The fast growth in business services is expected to continue. Temporary help agencies are also expected to expand as more companies try to meet cyclical changes without hiring more employees.[6]

---

[5] See Wayne J. Howe, "The Business Services Industry Sets Pace in Employment Growth," *Monthly Labor Review,* April 1986.
[6] Valerie A. Personick, "A Second Look at Industry Output and Employment Trends through 1995," *Monthly Labor Review,* November 1985.

Employment Implications

What does the expanding service economy offer American workers? As the traditional blue-collar jobs are replaced through automation or are "exported" to other countries where manufacturers can produce their goods at lower cost, displaced workers must enter new occupations or join the jobless ranks. Displaced workers — who represent about 14 percent of the unemployed — may find help in locating new jobs through Title III of the Job Training Partnership Act (JTPA, PL 97-300), which Congress passed in 1982 at the peak of the recession. The first federal program aimed at displaced workers since the early 1960s, JTPA took effect in October 1983 when the states initiated job placement and retraining programs funded under Title III.

The effectiveness of the law has been brought into question, however. A recent study conducted by the Office of Technology Assessment (OTA), a research organization of the U.S. Congress, found that less than 5 percent of the eligible people had enrolled in the program by mid-1985. It also reported that the states participating in the program had emphasized job placement but did little to retrain displaced workers who had held menial jobs. A particular failing of the program, according to the study, is the lack of remedial education. Many displaced factory workers are functional illiterates who lack "the basic skills which would qualify them for good new jobs or for training in skilled occupations." [7]

But even if federally supported retraining programs are improved, an unlikely event in a era of federal spending cuts, still more workers are expected to be squeezed out of the goods-producing economy. Technological advances will continue to foster the development of new kinds of manufacturing industries but, the OTA study concluded, "high-technology manufacturing sectors, such as computer and semiconductor manufacture, are unlikely to rescue many workers displaced from traditional manufacturing sectors."

Nor is the service sector an attractive alternative to manufacturing for many Americans. The study found that pay is lower in service-producing industries than in manufacturing for production and non-supervisory workers: an average of $7.52 vs. $9.18 an hour in 1984, the last year of comparison. Many observers say the shift toward services is bringing about a decline in

---

[7] Congress of the United States, Office of Technology Assessment, "Technology and Structural Unemployment: Reemploying Displaced Adults," February 1986, p. 18.

9

the standard of living for many Americans, and not just workers displaced from traditional manufacturing jobs. Technological progress is expected to diminish the need for stenographers, truck and tractor drivers, telephone station installers and repairers, and statistical clerks. There will also be less demand for farmers, railroad workers, household workers, and production workers in such declining industries as textiles and footwear. At the same time, demand will increase for computer programmers, computer systems analysts, as well as electrical and electronics engineers and technicians. Health-related occupations are also expected to stay in heavy demand as the elderly represent an ever larger portion of the population.

The prospects for employment in the service-based economy are especially grim for older blue-collar workers. "These people are in real trouble," said Thierry Noyelle of Columbia University's Conservation of Human Resources Project. "Nothing will ever happen to them but to vanish into retirement." Another group at greater risk than blue-collar workers in general are high-school dropouts, who enter an increasingly skilled labor market without sufficient skills to find jobs. Noyelle contrasted this situation with the late 1960s, when the Vietnam War spurred demand for manufactured goods. Such a manufacture-driven economy, he explained, "could employ almost anyone who could wield a broom or a wrench." [8] He identifies a third group as underpaid or underemployed workers, who may have skills but are stuck in low-paid jobs.

Retraining is not the only problem. Primary training of workers entering the labor market for the first time has also undergone change in recent years. Whereas individual companies used to assume the burden of training employees on the job, Noyelle observed, this function has shifted to the educational system. "It used to be that a company would hire only a few managers with college degrees and train the rest who would be hired for entry-level positions," he said, "but this is no longer the case." A quarter of the workers aged 25 to 29 now hold degrees from four-year colleges, while only 10 percent did in 1960. As a result, businesses are able to recruit workers on various skill levels for "multiple entry points."

Once a worker could aspire to progress from an entry-level occupation to become president of the company. But Noyelle said career mobility is increasingly viewed as lateral rather than upward, at least at the middle and upper occupational levels. Instead of changing jobs within one company, he said, more employees seek progress within their professions, often through movement from company to company. High turnover may fur-

---

[8] All persons quoted in this report were interviewed by the author unless otherwise noted.

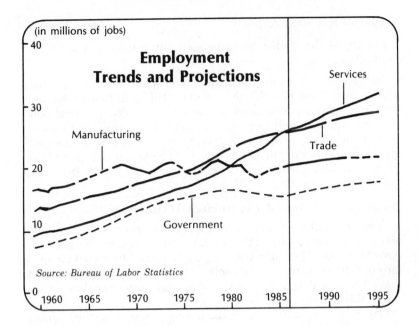

(in millions of jobs)

Employment Trends and Projections

Manufacturing

Services

Trade

Government

Source: Bureau of Labor Statistics

40 — 30 — 20 — 10 — 0

1960 1965 1970 1975 1980 1985 1990 1995

ther reduce an employer's interest in providing in-house training to workers.

The OTA study found that service industries tend to have both more low-paying and management jobs than manufacturing, whose workers are more likely to be unionized. Since few displaced factory workers have access to managerial positions, only the lower-paid occupations are likely to be open to them. Markley Roberts of the AFL-CIO speaks of the unwanted creation of a "two-tiered society" of rich and poor. Roberts, the labor federation's expert on service industries, said that although there are high-paying service jobs, "the expansion is occurring in the low-paid jobs." Projections by the Bureau of Labor Statistics on job growth support this notion: at least half of the 10 occupations expected to provide the most new jobs by 1995 are low in prestige and compensation.

While higher in prestige, two other fast-growing occupations — nursing and teaching (in kindergarten and elementary schools) — traditionally have been filled by women and have been poorly paid. Women, who have entered the work force in unprecedented numbers in the past two decades, have taken 65 percent of the new service jobs, according to the government study. Their entrance into the work place has in turn boosted consumer demand for all kinds of services once provided mostly by homemakers. Day-care centers, restaurants and other businesses have benefited and have also provided employment for women. But the service industries have not corrected the disparity in average earnings between men and women,[9] which at

---

[9] For background, see "Women's Economic Equity," *E.R.R.*, 1985 Vol. I, pp. 331-356.

64 cents to the dollar, remains virtually unchanged since the mid-1950s.

Service industries may provide a safer work environment than the factory floor. But the change may still be difficult for many workers. "For workers used to the social culture, physical conditions, hubbub, and noise of a factory, the transition to working in an office, health care facility, or restaurant is abrupt," said the authors of the OTA report. "The last major transition, from agricultural to manufacturing work, may have been less jolting for many people." [10]

Switch from Smokestacks to High Technology

The regional disparity in unemployment rates caused by the decline in basic manufacturing has not been corrected by the growth of service industries. In fact, while unemployment is around 10 percent in Michigan, where thousands of workers have been displaced from automobile and supporting industries, the jobless represent only 4 percent of the work force in Massachusetts, where high technology has absorbed many workers laid off from shoemaking and other traditional local manufacturing. High-tech manufacturing and computer-related service industries have thus far tended to be localized, as in California's Silicon Valley and around Boston, Mass. Even so, many companies cannot find enough electrical engineers and other qualified personnel for high-tech industries.

These centers of high-tech manufacturing and related business services are expected to continue to offer more jobs than other parts of the country. According to the National Planning Association, the Boston metropolitan area and three metropolitan areas in California — Los Angeles-Long Beach, Anaheim-Santa Ana, and San Jose — will provide the most new jobs in the country between 1985 and 2000. Houston, which ranked first in expected job growth in previous projections, fell to seventh place, an indication that the oil industry will not recover fully from its current crisis.[11]

Other changes in employment patterns are seen within metropolitan areas. The increasing use of computers and their integration into the telecommunications network have enabled more industries to abandon the inner cities, where traditional manufacturing has been concentrated, for the suburbs and outlying rural areas where real estate is cheaper. The result is a noticeable mismatch between job-seekers and job openings: unemployment among inner-city youth remains at double-digit

---

[10] Office of Technology Assessment, *op. cit.*, p. 155.

[11] Other metropolitan areas expected to offer the most jobs are, in descending order, Phoenix, Washington, Chicago, Dallas and Atlanta. The National Planning Association is a Washington-based research organization focusing on U.S. economic policy and international trade.

Most New Jobs, 1984-95
Increase in Thousands

Business services	2,633
Retail trade, except eating and drinking places	1,691
Eating and drinking places	1,203
Wholesale trade	1,088
Medical services	1,065
Professional services	1,040
New construction	558
Doctors' and dentists' services	540
Hotels and lodging places	385
Credit agencies and financial brokers	382

Source: Projection by Bureau of Labor Statistics

levels while help-wanted signs in the windows of suburban fast-food restaurants, convenience stores and other service establishments go unanswered.

Part of the problem is inadequate public transportation between the cities and the suburban work sites. A more important explanation is pay: urban job seekers may find that the cost of commuting is hardly covered by the wages offered by many service establishments. The categories of service industries with the most employees — retail trade and the service industries — pay on average just $5.92 per hour and $7.73 per hour, respectively, far below the $8.54 average hourly wage for production workers in the entire private sector.[12] Many entry-level jobs pay only the minimum wage of $3.35 an hour. Unchanged since 1981, the minimum wage has dropped in value by 18 percent when adjusted for inflation.

Some observers predict that the continuing mismatch between jobs and job-seekers may improve working conditions in the service economy. Retailers, who appear to be having the greatest trouble filling jobs, must offer higher wages and other benefits and hold out the promise of future promotion to attract entry-level workers to their establishments. "The trends are not so harmful as some have feared," wrote Janet L. Norwood, commissioner of Labor Statistics. "We can live with them if we have the flexibility to minimize the hardship associated with the changes and to capitalize on their potential benefits." [13]

But demographic changes mean these jobs may go unfilled for a long time. A "baby bust" of the late 1960s and early 1970s has thinned the ranks today of 16-24-year-olds, who make up the

---

[12] Bureau of Labor Statistics, "Employment and Earnings," September 1985.
[13] Writing in *The New York Times*, Aug. 28, 1985.

bulk of workers in fast-food restaurants and many other retail establishments. For those who already work bagging groceries or flipping hamburgers on the weekends and after school, there is a growing awareness of the harmful effects of working long hours at dead-end jobs: many working teenagers have been found to get behind in their studies or drop out of school altogether.[14] Without a diploma, few will have access to the training they need for better-paid service jobs, much less the graduate studies required for careers in the professions.

As a result, some companies have begun tapping the growing pool of potential job-seekers at the other extreme of the age spectrum, the retired. McDonald's — the world's largest fast-food chain — offers a two-week training program for workers 55 and older for employment in its restaurants. The "McMasters" program, initiated in Baltimore County, Md., is soon to expand to other areas of the country. This and other recruiting and training programs aimed at older Americans offer an incentive that is especially appealing to this age group, opportunities for part-time and temporary employment. Some training programs run by fast-food restaurants are geared toward the physically and mentally handicapped, who are less likely to quit out of boredom or low pay.

Unlike goods-producing industries, where a falloff in factory orders results in layoffs of full-time production workers, service industries are turning increasingly toward the use of temporary and part-time employees to meet demand during peak periods. According to Audrey Freedman of the Conference Board, there are about 700,000 such "contingent" workers now supplied by temporary help agencies, mostly in the service economy. No longer limited to offereng clerical help, temporary agencies are now providing doctors, lawyers, management consultants and other highly paid professionals to businesses and health-care facilities on a temporary basis. Temporary work is attractive to many professionals, either to gain a foothold in their professions or to keep working at a slower pace, whether in semi-retirement or out of choice in younger years.

Unions' Disadvantage in Service Economy

The shift toward services has been accompanied by a decline in union membership, as the labor movement has been less successful at organizing workers in service industries than it has in the goods-producing sectors. Roberts attributes the difficulty of organizing service workers to several factors. One is the resistance of many service employees to union representation. "There is a trend among white-collar workers to think they are on an upward track into management," he said, "even when the

---

[14] See *The Wall Street Journal*, May 27, 1986.

reality of their employment should tell them that's a misguided view." Another obstacle is the high expense involved in organizing campaigns in service establishments, which — with the exception of large hospitals and universities — are smaller than goods-producing firms.

Roberts explained that a high proportion of service sector workers are women, members of minority groups and young people, all especially susceptible to exploitation at the work place. The frustration and discontent felt among these employees, he said, should make union organizing easier, but this situation also leads to high labor turnover, a drawback in any organizing campaign. An important obstacle to union penetration in the services, Roberts added, is widespread anti-union activities on the part of employers — "union-busting in industries where unions exist, blocking unions where they don't."

This is not to say that unions have made no inroads. Roberts noted that the fastest-growing unions affiliated with the AFL-CIO are the Service Employees International Union (SEIU), United Food and Commercial Workers International Union and the American Federation of State, County and Municipal Employees (AFSCME), which have concentrated their organizing efforts among clerical, retail and government employees, respectively. Still, Roberts conceded, "we have a long way to go. Despite a lot of soul-searching on the part of labor as to the best ways to go about organizing the services, it's not easy."

U.S. Competitiveness

The service industries themselves are not solely responsible for the shift toward a service economy. In response to growing international competition for their products, manufacturers are diversifying their operations to provide services, thus boosting the number of service jobs within the manufacturing sector. At the same time, manufacturers are continuing to "outsource," shifting production — and manufacturing jobs — to other countries where labor costs are lower.

This trend has fed concerns that American businesses are becoming "hollow corporations," dealing in all aspects of the creation and selling of a product except production itself.[15] In this view, Americans are rapidly passing from an era of industrialization, to one of de-industrialization, in which manufacturing jobs are exported offshore, and ultimately to a post-industrial society, in which manufacturing no longer holds a

---

[15] See, for example, "The Hollow Corporation," *Business Week,* March 3, 1986.

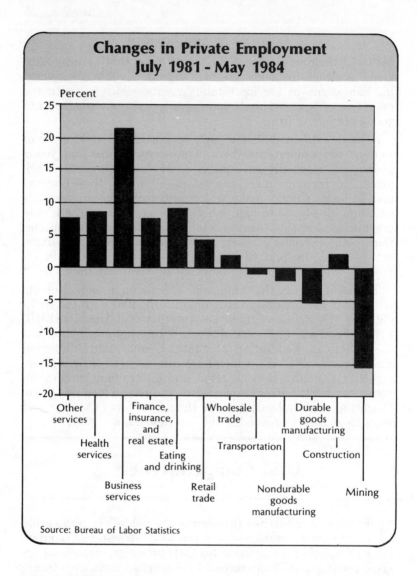

**Changes in Private Employment
July 1981 - May 1984**

Percent

Categories (left to right):
Other services, Health services, Business services, Finance, insurance, and real estate, Eating and drinking, Retail trade, Wholesale trade, Transportation, Nondurable goods manufacturing, Durable goods manufacturing, Construction, Mining

Source: Bureau of Labor Statistics

significant place. The authors of the federal study on trade in services de-emphasize the impact this shift will have on employment. "The growth of services is not job-destroying any more than the shift from an agricultural to an industrial economy was," they wrote. [16]

But labor leaders and economists who have urged the formulation of a federal industrial policy to restore the health of U.S. goods-producing industries fear this transformation will have a disastrous outcome. Low-level clerical jobs, including data-entry jobs, have already been moving offshore for the past 20 years. The Office of Technology Assessment reported in

---

[16] Office of the U.S. Trade Representative, *op. cit.*, p. 10.

December 1985, in fact, that American firms employ some 5,000 workers overseas to do data-entry work, some 2,300 of them in the Caribbean area. What some experts fear is that the fast-growing, higher-level occupations will follow.

In calling for an industrial policy, Robert B. Reich, professor of business and public policy at Harvard University, warned that ". . . the nation cannot rely on services. America's sales of services depend on the vigor of its future manufacturing base." Such services as banking, engineering, legal and insurance services are so closely linked to the production of goods, he argued, that they will follow the assembly-line overseas.[17]

But researchers at Columbia University's Conservation of Human Resources Project have come to a less pessimistic conclusion. "The shift to services is neither de-industrialization nor post-industrialization, but something in between," argued Thierry Noyelle. In his view, the shift toward services is not unlike the shift from agriculture to manufacturing. During that time farm employment decreased while farm output increased through mechanization. "The same thing is happening now," Noyelle said. "Employment in manufacturing is declining, but the value of manufacturing output will continue to increase" as new services boost productivity. "We say the growth of services is a complement to manufacturing." Noyelle noted that in the auto industry robots replace auto-production workers, but white-collar workers and engineers produce and operate the robots. "The industry will still be cranking out cars, it's just the way it does it that will be different," he said.

Pursuing the Global Market: U.S. vs. Japan

The shift toward services is also occurring in other industrialized countries, although not as extensively as in the United States. Service industries represent 59 and 57 percent of the economies of France and Japan, respectively, according to BLS figures. Services also are assuming a growing role in international trade. A study by the Committee for Economic Development found that international trade in services not only had doubled in volume between 1974 and 1984 but was becoming increasingly diversified: "No longer do services simply support traded goods (e.g., shipping and freight insurance). Some services now lead goods (e.g., information services often lead computer sales); others, such as accounting, essentially have nothing to do with goods. In short, trade in services has not only been growing rapidly but also has assumed a high degree of importance in its own right."[18]

---

[17] Robert B. Reich, *The Next American Frontier* (1983), p. 132.

[18] Committee for Economic Development, "Strategy for U.S. Industrial Competitiveness," April 19, 1984, pp. 166-167. The committee is a New York-based research organization that studies national policy issues.

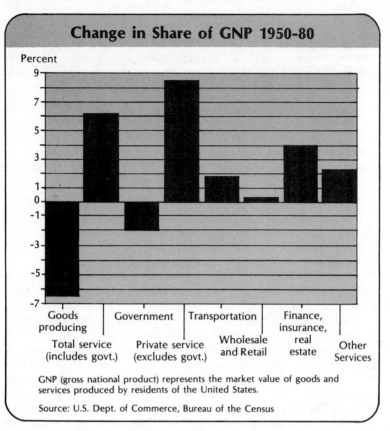

Change in Share of GNP 1950-80

Percent

GNP (gross national product) represents the market value of goods and services produced by residents of the United States.

Source: U.S. Dept. of Commerce, Bureau of the Census

Although the United States remains the largest exporter of services and has enjoyed a sizable trade surplus in services, this advantage has shrunk in recent years, from $28.1 billion in 1983 to $21.4 billion in 1985. Japan, long a target of protectionist sentiment because of its surpluses in merchandise trade with the United States, is now coming under scrutiny for allegedly restricting imports of American services. Sen. Frank H. Murkowski, R-Alaska, told a congressional panel that the U.S. service trade with Japan dropped from a surplus of $1.3 billion in 1982 to a deficit of $1.8 billion in 1985.[19]

Congress is coming under pressure this election year from constituents to do something about the trade deficit. On May 22, the House passed a bill (HR 4800) that would require the president to force countries found to discriminate against American imports to cut their trade surpluses with the United States by 10 percent a year.[20] A less restrictive bill before the Senate Finance Committee would also allow the president less

[19] Remarks at hearings on the U.S.-Japan services trade held June 5, 1986, by the Senate Foreign Relations Subcommittee on East Asian and Pacific Affairs, which he chairs.
[20] For background, see Steven Pressman, "Over Reagan's Protest, House Votes Trade Bill," *Congressional Quarterly Weekly Report*, May 24, 1986.

discretion than he now enjoys in deciding what measures to take to correct trade imbalances.

The Reagan administration is eager to keep protectionism from undermining a new round of negotiations under the General Agreement on Tariffs and Trade (GATT), expected to begin this fall. But it is planning to push for the liberalization of trade in services and its inclusion in GATT regulations, which currently cover only those services directly tied to trade in goods. Thierry Noyelle disputes the contention that the United States is at a disadvantage in services trade and listed such growing fields as software, data processing, accounting, advertising, legal services and management consulting as ones clearly dominated by U.S. firms.

Nor is that advantage likely to wane in Noyelle's view. Computerization, he said, will allow U.S. industry to rationalize production and restore competitiveness to the goods-producing sector. Meanwhile, the shift to services is changing the traditional emphasis from the production of goods to their distribution. Companies selling computer software, for example, must custom-design their products according to the buyer's needs. Noyelle added that Japan, America's biggest competitor in computer hardware, is "backward" when it comes to selling software. International competition will hinge on which country's industry understands first what the market wants and delivers the product the fastest. And no country, in his view, is better suited to compete on this ground than the United States, where "marketing and sales people are actually in the driver's seat" in many companies.

Recommended Reading List

Books

Bluestone, Barry, and Bennett Harrison, *The Deindustrialization of America*, Basic Books, 1982.

Noyelle, Thierry J., and Thomas M. Stanback Jr., *The Economic Transformation of American Cities*, Rowman & Allanheld, 1983.

Reich, Robert B., *The Next American Frontier*, Penguin Books, 1983.

Stanback, Thomas M. Jr., et al., *Services: The New Economy*, Rowman & Allanheld, 1981.

Articles

Business Week, selected articles.

Howe, Wayne J., "The Business Services Industry Sets Pace in Employment Growth," *Monthly Labor Review,* April 1986.

Kutscher, Ronald E., and Valerie A. Personik, "Deindustrialization and the Shift of Services," *Monthly Labor Review,* June 1986.

Louis, Arthur M., "America's New Economy," *Fortune,* June 23, 1986.

Nasar, Sylvia, "Jobs Go Begging at the Bottom," *Fortune,* March 17, 1986.

Personick, Valerie A., "A Second Look at Industry Output and Employment Trends through 1995," *Monthly Labor Review,* November 1985.

Reports and Studies

AFL-CIO Committee on the Evolution of Work, "The Future of Work," August 1983.

Committee for Economic Development, "Strategy for U.S. Industrial Competitiveness," April 19, 1984.

Freedman, Audrey, "Perspectives on Employment," Conference Board, May 5, 1986.

Office of Technology Assessment, "Technology and Structural Unemployment: Reemploying Displaced Adults," February 1986.

Terleckyj, Nestor E., "Regional Economic Growth in the United States: Projections for 1985-2000," NPA (National Planning Association) National Data Services, Inc., June 1986.

U.S. Department of Commerce, Bureau of the Census, "1984 Service Annual Survey," August 1985.

U.S. Department of Labor, Bureau of Labor Statistics, "Employment and Earnings," March 1986.

—— "Employment, Hours, and Earnings, United States, 1909-84, Vol. II," March 1985.

U.S. Trade Representative, "U.S. National Study on Trade in Services: a Submission by the United States Government to the General Agreement on Tariffs and Trade," 1984.

Graphics: Charts pp. 5,7,11,13,16,18, staff artists; p. 1 illustration by Richard Pottern.

WORKING ON WELFARE

by

Robert K.
Landers

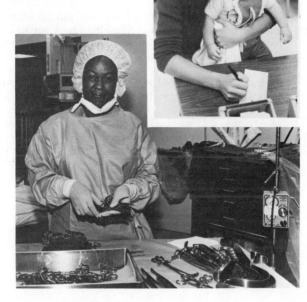

**Oct. 10
1 9 8 6**

Editor's Note: Since this report was published, welfare reform gained further attention in Washington. A broad consensus has emerged on the need to link work and welfare. This was apparent in reports issued by such groups as the National Governors' Association, the Working Seminar on the Family and American Welfare Policy, headed by Michael Novak of the American Enterprise Institute for Public Policy Research; and the Project on the Welfare of Families, headed by former Gov. Bruce E. Babbit of Arizona, a Democratic presidential candidate, and Arthur S. Fleming, secretary of Health, Education and Welfare under President Eisenhower. Congress was actively trying in the spring of 1987 to translate this broad consensus into legislative reality.

The Underclass, Welfare and Work

Journalist Bill Moyers with jobless father Timothy McSeed.

Scenes from a ghetto.

Scene One:

Alice Sondra Jackson, a 23-year-old unmarried mother, living in Newark, N.J., and pregnant with her third child, tells journalist Bill Moyers: *"I don't think I would have had the second two children, if I didn't think welfare was there. I don't like welfare because it makes me lazy."*

Bill Moyers: *"It does?"*

Jackson: *"Yeah, it makes you lazy just to sit around and wait for a monthly check to come in. You know, I just like to work; I like money coming every week or every two weeks."*

Scene Two:

Timothy McSeed, the unemployed, 26-year-old father of Jackson's children and of three others by as many other women

Poverty, Dysfunction Define the Underclass

There is close agreement among experts about the nature of what has come to be called the underclass, reports political scientist Lawrence M. Mead. The underclass, he writes in *Beyond Entitlement*, "comprises those Americans who *combine* relatively low income with functioning problems such as difficulties in getting through school, obeying the law, working, and keeping their families together.

"These characteristics, in turn, are traceable to an unstable family life, marked by absent fathers, erratic parenting, and low self-esteem and aspiration. . . .

"The underclass is most visible in urban slum settings and is about 70 percent nonwhite, but it includes many rural and white people as well, especially in Appalachia and the South. Much of the urban underclass is made up of street hustlers, welfare families, drug addicts, and former mental patients. There are, of course, needy people who function well — the so-called 'deserving' or 'working poor' — and better off people who function poorly, but in general low income and serious behavioral difficulties go together. The underclass is not large as a share of population, perhaps 9 million people, but it accounts for the lion's share of the most serious disorders in American life, especially in the cities." *

* *Lawrence M. Mead*, Beyond Entitlement: The Social Obligations of Citizenship *(1985), p. 22.*

— none of whom he supports: *"Well, the majority of the mothers are on welfare. And welfare gives them the stipend for the month. So what I'm not doing, the government does."*

Broadcast early this year, Moyers' two-hour CBS documentary, *The Vanishing Family: Crisis in Black America*, was powerful television journalism, and it was much discussed. For the first time, a mass audience got a close look at what has come

Liberals and conservatives are revising their thinking about welfare and work.

to be called the underclass, that troubled and troublesome fraction of the poor whose millions of members have great difficulty functioning in accordance with the norms of the larger society. (*See box, opposite page.*) Moyers had been a special assistant to President Johnson when "war" was declared on poverty in 1964. Now, he was, in effect, conveying to millions of viewers the news that the liberal wisdom on the subject of welfare and poverty was being revised. Illegitimacy and welfare dependency were important problems, after all, and not mere phantasms useful for "blaming the victim."

Liberals are not the only ones who have been revising their thoughts about welfare and poverty in recent years. Conservatives, too, have been rethinking their approach to the subject. They have put new stress on the impact of welfare dependency and non-work on the poor, rather than the impact of welfare expenditures on government budgets or the need to eliminate welfare fraud.

Reagan Report on Welfare 'Crisis'

Aid to Families with Dependent Children (AFDC) is the principal welfare program and, indeed, what most people mean when they speak of welfare. The federal government contributes more than half of AFDC's total cost (about $15 billion in 1985), but the states, operating within federal guidelines, administer the cash-payment program, determine eligibility standards and set benefit levels.

The program began as a New Deal effort to assist widows with small children; such women were not expected to work outside

Poverty/Spending Paradox

Federal Cash Public Assistance (in billions)   **Millions of Persons Under Poverty Line**

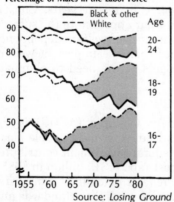

Source: *Losing Ground*

Trends in Social Functioning

Year	Recipients of AFDC (thousands)	Unemployment rate (percent)	Serious Crimes (thousands)
'60	3,005	5.4	3,384
'65	4,329	4.4	4,739
'70	8,466	4.8	8,098
'75	11,346	8.3	11,257
'80	10,774	7.0	13,295
'81	11,079	7.5	13,290
'82	10,358	9.5	12,857
'83	10,761	9.5	12,070

Source: *Beyond Entitlement*

Workforce Participation Gap
Percentage of Males in the Labor Force

Source: *Losing Ground*

Note: Breaks in poverty line indicate calculation revisions. AFDC is aid to families with dependent children.

the home. By the late 1950s, however, it had become widely apparent that most AFDC recipients were not widows; many had never even been married and many still were continuing to have more children. Welfare was becoming for some a permanent way of life.

During the 1960s, legislative, administrative and court decisions transformed the welfare system; welfare began to be regarded as a right. AFDC was made more generous and less restrictive, and new programs, such as food stamps and Medicaid (health-care insurance for the poor), were added. Between 1965 and 1970, the AFDC caseload mushroomed by 125 percent. By 1985, nearly 3.7 million families — most of them headed by women who were separated or divorced or never married — were receiving AFDC cash payments.[1] In return for their benefits, recipients generally were required to do very little.

Although the extent of chronic welfare dependency is a matter of definition and scholarly dispute, the problem is increasingly

[1] During the early years of the Reagan administration, certain changes were made in AFDC and other welfare programs that slowed their growth. President Reagan insisted that the "social safety net" was still in place for the "truly needy." His critics derided that contention and said the poor were being hurt. See "Social Welfare Under Reagan," *E.R.R.*, 1984 Vol. I, pp. 189-208.

being recognized as a significant one, not least for those in the underclass. In addition, with almost half the mothers in the country with children under 3 working outside the home, there is an increasingly widespread disposition to think that welfare mothers should not necessarily be exempt from work. And so there seems to be a new consensus in the making about the need to link welfare and work. The result may be a new effort, more serious than in the past, to forge that link.

In his State of the Union address last February, President Reagan declared: "In the welfare culture, the breakdown of the family, the most basic support system, has reached crisis proportions — in female and child poverty, child abandonment, horrible crimes and deteriorating schools. After hundreds of billions of dollars in poverty programs, the plight of the poor grows more painful. But the waste in dollars and cents pales before the most tragic loss — the sinful waste of human spirit and potential."

Reagan — whose 1971 California Welfare Reform Act has been described as the "proudest achievement in the eight years of his governorship" [2] — said he was directing the White House Domestic Council to present him by Dec. 1 with "an evaluation of programs and a strategy for immediate action to meet the financial, educational, social, and safety concerns of poor families. I am talking about real and lasting emancipation, because the success of welfare should be judged by how many of its recipients become independent of welfare."

To the disappointment of some outside the Reagan administration, the White House did not appoint a blue-ribbon commission to take up the matter of welfare reform, but gave the job instead to several inconspicuous working groups within the administration. One group, headed by Charles D. Hobbs, director of the White House Office of Policy Development, is looking primarily at low-income assistance programs; a second group, headed by Education Under Secretary Gary L. Bauer, is focusing on the state of the American family.[3] A third group, headed by Assistant Attorney General Charles J. Cooper, has been examining the subject of federalism for more than a year. According to an administration official involved, the federalism group is concentrating on "process" rather than on specific programs and so is taking "a very different approach" from

---

[2] Lou Cannon, *Reagan* (1982), p. 182. However, Gov. Reagan's California Work Experience Program for welfare recipients, which, David L. Kirp, a professor of public policy at the University of California (Berkeley) has written "was supposed to deliver 30,000 jobs, at its peak managed only slightly more than 1,000 placements, many of them jobs invented by government itself." See Kirp, "The California Work/Welfare Scheme, *The Public Interest*, spring 1986, p. 39.

[3] See "New Deal for the Family," p. 85

Reagan's 1982 New Federalism initiative. Under that plan, the federal government would have transferred its responsibility for the AFDC and food stamp programs to the states in exchange for assuming the full cost of Medicaid. The proposal aroused strong objections from state and local officials, and Congress did nothing about New Federalism.

Although a blue-ribbon panel on welfare reform was not appointed by the White House, one whose composition might have been acceptable to Reagan came into existence anyway: the Working Seminar on the Family and American Welfare

"To make welfare more demanding will achieve much more than further fiddling with benefits and incentives," says political scientist Lawrence M. Mead.

Policy, headed by Michael Novak, a resident scholar at the conservative American Enterprise Institute for Public Policy Research (AEI). The seminar, said Novak last July when its formation was announced, "will seek new directions in family and welfare policy reform. It will try to bring the beginnings of a new consensus to the public debate."

Sponsored by Marquette University's Institute for Family Studies, under grants from the Lynde and Harry Bradley Foundation and the John M. Olin Foundation, the seminar counts several former administration officials (including former United Nations Representative Jeane J. Kirkpatrick) among its members. It also boasts such scholars as Charles Murray, author of the much praised and much criticized book, *Losing Ground: American Social Policy, 1950-1980,* and Lawrence M. Mead, author of *Beyond Entitlement: The Social Obligations of Citizenship,* a book that has begun to attract some national attention.

According to panel member Leslie Lenkowsky, who is president of the Institute for Educational Affairs, a conservative foundation, the "reasonably bipartisan" seminar will be making a report in time to contribute to "what we expect will be a debate on the subject next year in Congress."

Vigorous Debate on Welfare Reform

The existence of this high-powered panel helps to ensure that there will be, in fact, a vigorous public debate about welfare reform, after the administration task forces make their reports. Indeed, to some extent, that debate, spurred by *Losing Ground* and Moyers' documentary, has already begun.

Journalists Nicholas Lemann of *The Atlantic* and Mickey Kaus of *The New Republic* have created stirs recently with their respective analyses. Lemann has emphasized the role of a "separate, self-sustaining culture" in keeping people in the underclass, and suggested that the government should undertake "a major national effort with the clear-eyed goal of acculturation." Kaus has argued that cash or cash-like welfare for the able-bodied — single-parents included — should be halted and that the government instead should offer public-sector, sub-minimum-wage jobs to any able-bodied citizen over 18 who wants one.[4]

New York University political scientist Mead contended in his book, published in late 1985, that low-skilled jobs in the private sector are already widely available and that the government should require welfare recipients to work as a civic obligation. "To make welfare *more demanding*," he told a House of Representatives committee last spring, "will achieve much more than further fiddling with benefits and incentives."[5]

Many states in recent years — from Massachusetts, with its much-publicized Employment and Training Choices program (ET), to California, with its Greater Avenues for Independence

California's Greater Avenues for Independence program is an effort to link welfare with work.

(GAIN)[6] — have undertaken in various ways, mostly small, to link welfare with work. The Manpower Demonstration Research Corp., a non-profit social science research organization, is

---

[4] See Lemann, "The Origins of the Underclass," *The Atlantic,* June 1986, pp. 31-55, and July 1986, pp. 54-68; and Lemann, "Ghettos: What Has to Be Done," *The Washington Post,* Sept. 8, 1986, p. A15. Also see Kaus, "The Work Ethic State," *The New Republic,* July 7, 1986, pp. 22-33, and Kaus *et al.,* "Welfare & Work: A Symposium," *The New Republic,* Oct. 6, 1986, pp. 18-23.

[5] Mead testified before the House Select Committee on Children, Youth, and Families, on April 17.

[6] See Kirp, *op. cit.,* and Kaus, *op. cit.*

conducting a five-year, 11-state study of such "work initiatives." Earlier this year, the organization issued an interim report on pilot programs in San Diego, Calif., Baltimore, Md., and two Arkansas counties; it found they had produced modest gains in employment.

In the developing debate over welfare reform, the administration does not have the political stage to itself. Indeed, it appears

Former Virginia Democratic Gov. Charles S. Robb has called for "a new targeted offensive on joblessness, dependency and poverty."

that the stage is becoming quite crowded with political leaders:

● Former Virginia Gov. Charles S. Robb, who is chairman of the Democratic Leadership Council and has been mentioned as a possible candidate on the 1988 Democratic national ticket, addressed the problems posed by the underclass in a speech at Hofstra University last April. He called for "a new, targeted offensive on joblessness, dependency and poverty."

Robb, son-in-law of President Johnson, said the original emphasis of Johnson's Great Society programs "on self-help and community action has given way to a large and paternalistic welfare bureaucracy which sees recipients as helpless victims rather than as citizens in need of help." Indeed, the welfare system, Robb said, "seems to be subsidizing the spread of self-destructive behavior in our poor communities." It is necessary, he argued, "to restore the balance between the entitlements and the obligations of citizenship" and to undertake more workfare initiatives like Massachusetts' ET. In a speech in September in Charleston, S.C., Robb cited Mead and his book as having defined "the basic social obligations that we should expect of welfare recipients, just as we expect them from all citizens."

● House Democrats weighed in last July with a report — "The Road to Independence: Strengthening America's Families in Need." The House Democratic Caucus' Social Policy Task Force, headed by Reps. Buddy MacKay of Florida and Marcy Kaptur of Ohio, asserted in the report that it is "not appropriate" to require mothers of preschool children to take part in work-related programs, but that many such mothers might choose to do so voluntarily. The task force said the focus now should be "on how best to design" employment and training programs "so that they are most effective in breaking down employment barriers and moving recipients into regular, wage-paying jobs — particularly the long-term recipients who now spend years in the underclass."

● The National Governors' Association has a committee (headed by its new president, Gov. Bill Clinton, D-Ark., and Gov. Michael N. Castle, R-Del.) at work, trying to devise a plan for reducing welfare dependency through expanded job-training efforts and other measures. "The cornerstone of the plan is prevention," the governors said in a resolution unanimously adopted in August.

● And Arizona Gov. Bruce E. Babbitt, who has been mentioned as a possible 1988 Democratic presidential candidate, is co-chairing another study group, the Project on the Welfare of Families. (His co-chairman is Arthur S. Fleming, who served as Health, Education and Welfare secretary during the latter years of the Eisenhower administration.) This group, some of whose members also belong to the Working Seminar on the Family and American Welfare Policy, is expected to issue an interim report in early December.

It seems, then, that in the months ahead there will be no shortage of studies, reports, speeches and proposals devoted to changing the welfare system and aiding those in the underclass. Lenkowsky, who is a former adviser to Sen. Daniel Patrick Moynihan, D-N.Y., and has written about welfare reform, said that "as society becomes more prosperous, as economic times are good, there's a heightened interest in the poor and the dependent. And that's what we've been seeing. I think about every 25 years, the poor are rediscovered. And we're now in the process of a rediscovery of the poor." To what extent the poor in the underclass benefit from this rediscovery remains to be seen.

'Losing Ground' in the War

In Michael Harrington's *The Other America: Poverty in the United States*, the 1962 book that eventually came to the attention of President Kennedy and helped inspire what became Johnson's "war on poverty," Harrington wrote that "the new poverty" — in which, by his count, 40-50 million people were then sunk — "is so constructed as to destroy aspiration; it is a system designed to be impervious to hope. . . . Poverty in the

Charles Murray's "Losing Ground" sparked debate.

United States is a culture, an institution, a way of life. . . . The family structure of the poor, for instance, is different from that of the rest of the society. There are more homes without a father, there is less marriage, more early pregnancy and . . . markedly different attitudes toward sex. As a result of this . . . hundreds of thousands, and perhaps millions, of children in the other America never know stability and 'normal' affection." It was up to "the larger society, with its help and resources" to "make it possible for these people to help themselves."

Twenty-two years and one official war on poverty later, the socialist author announced in a new book: "The poor are still there." In *The New American Poverty* (1984), Harrington argued that the war in Vietnam had subverted the war on poverty, which in consequence became little more than a "skirmish," albeit a modestly worthwhile one. More recently, the poor had been battered by a technological revolution and by foreign trade competition that eliminated many jobs and began to reshape the U.S. economy. Thanks to these "massive international and national trends," Harrington argued, there were "new structures of misery" and "a new poverty much more tenacious than the old."

To abolish this new poverty, he argued, a full-employment economy was required, along with some "fairly radical changes" to bring it about. Those changes would include more extensive economic planning and a "redistribution of income and wealth." A full-fledged national health-care program would greatly assist the working poor, and "serious job training programs" and child care would help bring the members of the underclass "back into the community."

Harrington's vision was a humane one in intent, but to many one-time sympathizers, it was no longer persuasive. His 1984 tract occasioned no great excitement; his summons to embark upon a "pilgrimage toward the fullness of our humanity" evoked little response. The poor were still there, but the old answers as to what should be done for them no longer seemed entirely adequate.

And so along came Murray with *Losing Ground,* and a thesis about the poor that contrasted sharply with Harrington's. As Murray put it in an interview, he "lanced a boil that had been festering for a while. There were just lots and lots of people who still paid lip service to the catechism about, well, it's-the-fault-of-continuing-racism, it's-the-fault-of-not-creating-enough-jobs, it's-the-fault-of-inadequate-effort-on-the-government's-part. They still recited all of that, [but] they didn't really believe it anymore. So the timing was right."

Indeed it was. Published in late 1984, Murray's book attracted an enormous amount of attention and, before many months had passed, strenuous attempts at rebuttal from various liberal redoubts. Murray unquestionably had struck a nerve, and *Losing Ground* became much more than a book. Harrington complained that it had turned into "a kind of political magic wand which conservatives wave when they want to make the arguments of their opponents disappear." *Newsweek* columnist Meg Greenfield said the effect of the book had been profound: "No matter what kind of government effort you may argue for these days in this area, and no matter what obligation, be it ever so modest, you may say the government should assume, you are likely to be 'Charles Murrayed,' and that will be the end of the argument. The simple invocation of the book's existence will be taken as an answer to the question, even as an implied 'policy choice.' " [7]

The initial reviews of *Losing Ground,* Murray recalled, "ranged from respectful to, in the case of Nick Lemann, quite positive, in his early review in *The New Republic,* which Nick Lemann told me subsequently, earned him more enmity among some of his friends than any review he'd ever done. And then shortly thereafter, came the [Robert] Greenstein article in *The New Republic* and [Christopher] Jencks [in *The New York Review of Books*] and Harrington [in *The New Republic*]. You could almost feel people out there saying, 'People are thinking

---

[7] Harrington, "Crunched Numbers," *The New Republic,* Jan. 28, 1985, p. 7; Greenfield, *Newsweek,* Feb. 11, 1985, p. 80.

this guy's right. We've got to stop that. It's getting too important.' "[8]

The Man Behind a Controversial Book

One reason *Losing Ground* attracted so much notice was Murray himself. He did not seem to be a cold-hearted, balance-the-budget-on-the-backs-of-the-poor sort. And he wasn't. As an undergraduate at Harvard University in the early 1960s, the young man from Newton, Iowa, had admired Kennedy and found conservative William F. Buckley Jr.'s magazine, *National Review*, extremely irritating. He voted for Johnson in 1964, regarding the conservative alternative, Sen. Barry Goldwater, as less than a credible candidate. While at Harvard, Murray had tried to "do good," working, for example, as a volunteer in a mental hospital. After graduation, he joined the Peace Corps and went to Thailand, where he worked for two years in the Village Health and Sanitation Project. (Remarked Murray: "As a liberal arts graduate from Harvard, of course, I was a big expert on wells and privies.")

He married a Thai woman[9] and remained in Thailand until 1970, returning in 1972 to spend a sixth year there. In 1969, he went to work as a researcher for the American Institutes for Research, a non-profit social science research organization that evaluates U.S.-funded social programs. He worked first in Thailand, later in the United States. In Thailand, he said, "I became very thoughtful about a lot of these issues, when I went out to villages where people were extremely poor and saw all the ways in which their quality of life was not primarily dependent on how much money they had, and was not primarily dependent upon what the government did for them."

In the United States, Murray's work evaluating social programs ultimately turned out to be "a very frustrating profession. That's the reason I got out of it eventually. Because you kept documenting failure, and it got to be very depressing to document failures, including times when you had people working very hard, trying to make it go." In 1981, he left the American Institutes for Research, "jumping off the end of a cliff, in terms of my work," he said. He planned to support

---

[8] Lemann, "After The Great Society," *The New Republic*, Nov. 19, 1984, pp. 27-32; Harrington, *op. cit.*, pp. 7-10; Greenstein, "Losing Faith in *Losing Ground*," *The New Republic*, March 25, 1985, pp. 12-17; Jencks, "How Poor Are the Poor?," *The New York Review of Books*, May 9, 1985, pp. 41-49. See also Murray's exchange with Greenstein in "The Great Society: An Exchange," *The New Republic*, April 8, 1985, pp. 21-23; and Murray's exchange with Jencks in "*Losing Ground:* An Exchange," *The New York Review of Books*, Oct. 24, 1985, pp. 55-56. See also Sheldon Danziger and Peter Gottschalk, "The Poverty of *Losing Ground*," *Challenge*, May-June 1985, pp. 32-38, and David T. Ellwood and Lawrence H. Summers, "Is Welfare Really the Problem?," *The Public Interest*, spring 1986, pp. 57-78, along with Murray's rejoinder to Ellwood and Summers, "No, Welfare Isn't Really the Problem," *The Public Interest*, summer 1986, pp. 3-11.

[9] The marriage ended in divorce, after 13 years. Murray remarried and now lives in Washington, D.C.

himself by doing consulting work in evaluation, but he also wanted to do some writing. He solicited various research organizations for backing, and got just one positive response — from the Heritage Foundation. The monograph he did for Heritage ("Safety Nets and the Truly Needy: Rethinking the Social Welfare System") led to a fall 1982 article in *The Public Interest*, to the Manhattan Institute for Policy Research (where he is now a fellow) and to *Losing Ground*.

"I got to the point where I found myself occasionally having to go back and read the book," Charles Murray says of "Losing Ground."

Murray's argument in *Losing Ground* is a subtle one, and it has often been misconstrued. "I got to the point," he recalled, "where I found myself occasionally having to go back and read the book. I'm serious. I mean that absolutely literally. There were a couple of times I said, 'Wait a minute, you are defending something there which you never said.'" It was almost as if a second *Losing Ground*, a grossly simplified one, addressing subjects Murray did not address (such as the elderly poor) and containing statements he did not make (such as that increased welfare decreased employment) came into existence. "The *Losing Ground* of the headlines," Murray said, "is: 'Nothing works. Anything that government tries to do makes matters worse. And we ought to get rid of the entire social welfare system.' And I got caught up in that as much as anybody."

What Charles Murray Really Said

The book's subtitle, as Murray acknowledges, is somewhat misleading. The book is not a comprehensive examination of American "social policy" over three decades, as that term would ordinarily be understood. Nor is the book a kind of report card on all the legislated programs of the Great Society. Nor is it even a comprehensive evaluation of the government's efforts to eliminate poverty. The book is not concerned with the elderly poor, who, along with the rest of the elderly, were apparently assisted in recent decades by Medicare and Medicaid and by increased Social Security benefits, indexed to inflation. What *Losing Ground* is concerned with, as Murray stated in the first paragraph of the first chapter, is "the *working-aged* [his emphasis] poor and discriminated-against, not the elderly."

His argument in *Losing Ground* is, in essence, that the quality of life for the working-aged poor, and their children, took a turn for the worse in the 1960s, just when it would have been expected to take a turn for the better, and that this happened because the government, through its "social policy," changed the world of the poor and made it rational for them to behave in ways that were ultimately self-destructive.

Losing Ground is not a narrow anti-welfare screed. As Murray also explained in the first chapter, he chose the term "social policy" because he could not think of a better one. He rejected the term "welfare policy" as "far too narrow," and the broader term "social welfare policy" as still connoting the providing of "reified 'things' to people; and 'things' are only a small part of what government has given to the poor and disadvantaged." Murray then explained precisely what he meant by his chosen term: ". . . a loosely defined conglomeration of government programs, laws, regulations, and court decisions touching on almost every dimension of life. Welfare programs are part of social policy toward the poor, obviously. Jobs programs are part of social policy. So also are federal efforts to foster better health and housing among the disadvantaged. So also are the *Miranda* decision[10] and Affirmative Action and the Department of Education's regulations about bilingual education."

Murray's argument really had two parts. The first had to do with what happened. He pointed out that after two decades of progress in reducing poverty in America, improvement slowed in the late 1960s and stopped in the 1970s, and that this occurred "just as the public-assistance program budgets and the rate of increase in those budgets were highest." In addition, the lives of the working-aged poor began, in certain important respects, to get worse than, by any reasonable expectation, they should have, given the economic and social conditions prevailing in the society at large. The deterioration was manifested in increased joblessness, worsened education, more crime, and higher illegitimacy rates, especially among teenagers.

Thus, Murray noted in the book, in the late 1960s — "at the very moment when the [federal] jobs programs began their massive expansion" — the rate of unemployment among young black males started rising steeply, and the climb continued during the '70s. Young black males, when compared with young white males, "lost ground." Why? "The facile explanation — jobs for young blacks just disappeared, no matter how hard they

---

[10] In 1966, the Supreme Court ruled in *Miranda v. Arizona* that incriminating statements obtained in interrogating suspects could not be used by prosecutors unless strict procedures had been followed to make sure the individual was aware of his right to remain silent and to consult an attorney.

searched — runs into trouble," he wrote, "when it tries to explain the statistics on labor force participation." For, beginning even earlier, during the boom years of the mid-'60s, participation in the labor force by young black males began to decline substantially as compared with participation by young white males. (Persons who are not in the labor force are not only not employed: they are not actively looking for employment.) This deterioration in the job situation of young blacks took

Murray's book argues that government changed "the rules of the game" for the poor, making it "profitable" for them to behave destructively.

place just when "federal efforts to improve their position were most expensive and extensive — efforts not just in employment *per se*, but in education, health, welfare, and civil rights as well."

The question, of course, is why all this happened; Murray's answer was the second part of his argument. His contention, strongly argued but admittedly not proven, was that the government changed "the rules of the game" for the poor, making it "profitable" for them "to behave in the short term in ways that were destructive in the long term" and keeping those long-term losses hidden from view. Changes in welfare policy, in school rules, in sanctions for crime, all "pointed in the same direction," Murray wrote. "It was easier to get along without a job. It was easier for a man to have a baby without being responsible for it, for a woman to have a baby without having a husband. It was easier to get away with crime. Because it was easier for others to get away with crime, it was easier to obtain drugs. . . . Because it was easier to get along without a job, it was easier to ignore education. Because it was easier to get along without a job, it was easier to walk away from a job and thereby accumulate a record as an unreliable employee."

In addition, Murray argued, traditional moral distinctions among the poor themselves were eroded. The stigma was withdrawn from welfare, and the status previously accorded to the working poor was destroyed. "Means-tested" welfare programs, such as food stamps, Medicaid and housing assistance, in which eligibility for benefits is determined largely by income level, turned virtually all low-income persons into welfare recipients. The poor, whether working or not, came to be viewed as homogeneous: they were all victims, the "system" was at fault, and there was little they could do on their own to improve their situation. The working poor were thus permitted less pride, and the non-working poor were given less reason to work. For the working-aged poor and for their children, escape from poverty became less likely.

Losing Ground, Murray replied to one critic, "is not a call to the barricades for the radical right, and it is not an assault on our commitment to help the poor. It is a call to try to do better." [11]

Murray did not, in *Losing Ground*, attend to every significant aspect of his subject. "The thing that was finessed in the book and is very important," he said, "is the issue of culture. And this is why Nick Lemann, I think, is making a valuable contribution. Clearly, there are differences among different cultures in this country that explain part of what goes on." Lemann, in his *Atlantic* articles, "The Origins of the Underclass," has argued that the culture of the black underclass is rooted in the South of a generation ago. "In fact," Lemann wrote, "there seems to be a strong correlation between underclass status in the North and a family background in the nascent underclass of the sharecropper South."

In Lemann's analysis, one reason the figures for unemployment, poverty, and female-headed families in the ghettos have soared is the sudden exodus of middle-class and working-class blacks out of the ghettos in the late 1960s and '70s. "The 'losing ground' phenomenon, in which black ghettos paradoxically became worse during the time of the War on Poverty," Lemann wrote, "can be explained partly by the abrupt disappearance of all traces of bourgeois life in the ghettos and the complete social breakdown that resulted." In Lemann's view, "the greatest barrier" now standing in the way of progress by those in the black underclass is "the distinctive culture" of the underclass.

Work Obligation Seen Necessary

In the final chapter of *Losing Ground*, Murray proposed — as what he called a "thought experiment" — scrapping virtually all of the federal welfare and income-support structure for working-aged persons. "It would leave the working-aged per-

---

[11] Murray's reply to Greenstein in "The Great Society: An Exchange," *op. cit.*, p. 23.

son," he wrote, "with no recourse whatsoever except the job market, family members, friends, and public or private locally funded services. It is the Alexandrian solution: cut the knot, for there is no way to untie it." [12]

That, of course, as Murray readily acknowledges and indeed explicitly stated in his book, is not going to happen. For, as Lawrence Mead put it, such a solution is politically impossible: "The public wants to help the poor, even the employable poor, with some limitations," Mead said in an interview. "As a result, we just can't do what Murray wants." Moreover, Mead added, "I'm convinced, on my reading of the psychology of the poor and the existing work programs, that to simply expose them to the marketplace is not the best way to levy the work obligation. These are people who, by the very fact that they don't take the available jobs, are highly ambivalent about work, about functioning generally. And it isn't necessarily going to make them function any better just to throw them out into the cold."

· Murray and others, on both right and left, have attributed too much importance to economic incentives, in Mead's view; if the poor responded much to such incentives, they would not be poor. What the chronically dependent need, he said, is "an authoritative structure in welfare itself, where they are required to work, but they get the message not from the job market directly, but rather from the staff and also from other recipients. . . . And this gets a sharp response."

There is substantial agreement, Mead noted in *Beyond Entitlement*, about the social problem posed by the underclass and about the need to integrate that class into the larger society. But the debate between conservatives and liberals over how to accomplish that, he said, has been largely preoccupied with the size of government. Murray and others on the right contemplate getting rid of virtually all government welfare for the working-aged, while liberals and those further left would like to expand government assistance.

To Mead, this debate misses the point: "The main problem with the welfare state," he wrote in his book, "is not its size but its permissiveness, a characteristic that *both* liberals and conservatives seem to take for granted. The challenge to welfare statesmanship is not so much to change the extent of benefits as to couple them with serious work and other obligations that would encourage functioning and thus promote the integration of recipients. The goal must be to create for recipients *inside* the welfare state the same balance of support and expectation

---

[12] As the 'thought experiment' proceeded, he decided to reinstall unemployment insurance "in more or less its previous form."

that other Americans face *outside* it, as they work to support themselves and meet the other demands of society."

The work issue was, in Mead's view, what sent down to defeat such dramatic efforts at welfare reform as President Nixon's Family Assistance Plan, which was before Congress from 1969-72, and President Carter's Program for Better Jobs and Income, proposed in 1977. Both were guaranteed income proposals that provided recipients with incentives to work but did not require them to work. "Reform died, in essence," Mead wrote, "because conservatives and moderates demanded more onerous [work] requirements than liberals would accept." However, in the defeat of those reform efforts, he added, a new kind of welfare policy became visible: "Congress consistently rejected the extremes of either doing away with welfare for the employable or guaranteeing them an income. Instead most members wanted to preserve a generous welfare system, but also to require some kind of work performance by employable recipients."

Efforts in Past Limited, Ineffective

The federal government's efforts in the past to get states to link welfare and work have been limited and ineffective. States were first given authority to set up welfare/work programs in 1962, but few did so. In 1967, the Work Incentive (WIN) program was created to enable states to put employable AFDC recipients in work or training, but few states referred recipients to the program. In 1971, referrals were made mandatory, but most states still required only small proportions of registrants to participate actively in the WIN program. However, in 1981, while refusing to make "workfare" (in which able-bodied welfare recipients are obliged to work in return for benefits) a requirement, Congress did give states several options, including requiring welfare recipients to work. States were allowed to replace WIN with the Community Work Experience Program, in which AFDC recipients could be obliged to work in public or non-profit agencies in return for welfare benefits.

The Manpower Research Demonstration Corp. found that welfare/work demonstration projects in San Diego, Baltimore, and two counties in Arkansas produced some undramatic but significant gains in employment, when compared with results in control groups.[13] The projects involved mandatory job-search workshops and unpaid work experience for employable welfare applicants or recipients. Only Arkansas required participation by mothers with children under 6 (who make up the majority of welfare cases); the program proved as effective for those mothers as for ones whose children were older.

In San Diego, a program of mandatory job search, followed,

[13] The study is supported by a challenge grant from the Ford Foundation, with about half the funds for each state study coming from the states or local foundations.

for those still on welfare who did not find jobs, by about three months of unpaid work experience, increased quarterly employment rates by 3-8 percentage points above the rates for those in the control group. There were also modest changes in welfare dependency and benefit payments. Sixty-one percent of those in the experimental program were employed at some point during the follow-up period. However, a control group whose members did not take part in the job search/work experience program had 55 percent employed at some point during the follow-up period. Thus, the real gain produced by the experimental program was about 6 percent. Programs, however, "do not necessarily have to effect dramatic changes to be worthwhile," noted Judith M. Gueron, executive vice president of the manpower research group. "In fact small impacts can be significant if they are long-lasting or if they occur for a large number of people."

In San Diego, Baltimore and Arkansas, the experimental programs, when compared with the controls, had their greatest employment impacts on women who had little or no prior employment experience. That does not mean that they had the highest placement or post-program rates; in general, individuals with more employment experience did. However, as Gueron observed: "A program that achieves high placement rates by working with people who would have found jobs on their own or cycled off welfare anyway may look successful but not have accomplished much. In contrast, a program working with those who would have done very poorly on their own may look less successful (measured by placement or employment rates), but in fact it may have produced major changes in behavior." [14]

The most promising welfare/work programs, in Mead's view, are the ones in San Diego and West Virginia that have taken a "highly authoritative" stance. "They're helping people, but they're also demanding that they function," he said, citing the fact that more than half the welfare recipients in these programs were working. About Massachusetts' ET, Mead is "much more skeptical" because of its training-oriented and "permissive" nature. "It's voluntary, with the single requirement, I think, that if you're on welfare and your kids are over six, you have to register — but that's all." ET's proponents claim that since October 1983, it has moved 25,000 people off the welfare rolls and into jobs. However, no independent control group (of people not taking part in ET) has been set up, and so the program's putative success has not been rigorously tested. Mead thinks that, in reality, requiring only registration "isn't enough. You've got to push these people. If, in fact, opportunities were enough, they wouldn't be on welfare in the first place."

[14] Judith M. Gueron, "Work Initiatives For Welfare Recipients," Manpower Demonstration Research Corp., March 1986, pp. 22, 24.

A survey of welfare applicants in San Diego found that about four-fifths of those aware of the job-search requirement said it was fair, and that about 60-70 percent of those who knew of the work-experience requirement considered it fair. A Manpower Research Demonstration Corp. survey of participants in mandatory work-experience programs in five states found "the majority of participants in most of the states shared the view that a work requirement was fair." [15]

More Responsibility Urged for Recipients

The welfare-dependent, Mead observed, accept the idea that they should work, but more as aspiration than obligation. "That's their entire problem in life," he said: Their failure "to take responsibility for themselves. What you do by levying an obligation [to work or to prepare to work] is require them to take responsibility for something." The government needs to exercise "good, strong, legitimate authority, of the kind they ought to have had as children. . . . And the evidence is — and it's rather strong evidence, I think — that people respond to

[15] *Ibid.*, p. 13.

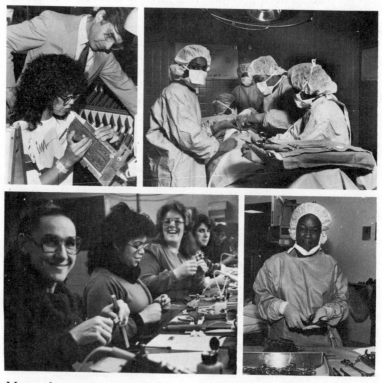

Massachusetts' employment and training program claims to have moved 25,000 people off welfare rolls and into jobs.

that, strongly and positively. One of the mysteries that is inexplicable to welfare activists who oppose a lot of work requirements is that the recipients feel positively about them."

There already are plenty of low-skilled jobs available in most areas of the country, Mead contends, and, were work to be made obligatory for welfare recipients, the government would need to provide only a small number of minimum wage jobs as a backup. Citing the "rapid progress of many recent immigrants" as evidence of the widespread availability of low-skilled jobs, Mead told Congress that the demand for low-skilled labor is so great "that some 5-10 million illegal aliens have entered the country to take jobs that unemployed Americans do not want."

And so, increasingly, it seems, the problem of the underclass is being understood not in terms of poverty, but in terms of people failing to function well. "In an odd sort of way," said Murray, "a lot of the things that I was saying have become conventional wisdom. And they have become conventional wisdom even among some of those who still consider that they oppose me and thought the book [*Losing Ground*] was rotten. . . . The whole acceptance of the existence of an underclass — which is not caused by the old culprits . . . [but which involves] a set of people who are behaving in ways that are absolutely nonsensical for them in the long run — well, that's a fairly major change in the way we perceive the problem."

That same distressing failure to function well was what Moyers' documentary showed so powerfully. The television program "made evident," Mead noted, "what is clear to all the analysts, which is, indeed, [that] dysfunctions, particularly illegitimacy and [non-]work, are the central reasons for poverty today. There's really no point in talking about poverty as a separate problem. . . . And what is and what is not 'functioning' is ultimately a political question: society decides what the common obligations are. One of them is to work; one of them is to obey the law. If these rules are violated, then a group comes under prejudice, whether or not it's poor. That's why we're now talking about the problem in these terms. And I think it's a step forward, because we're looking at the thing in the terms that now permit solutions. We're moving toward a solution."

But Mead does not envision the solution to be a panacea. The underclass would not instantly be made middle-class. Nor is it likely, in Mead's view, that the welfare rolls would be greatly reduced. "But what you can do, on the evidence we have," he said is "raise the proportion of people who are participating in something meaningful [to] over a half . . . of the employable [welfare] population. If we do that, we establish work as a norm on welfare, rather than non-work, and I think [that] over time, that will slowly have an effect on [the] welfare culture."

Recommended Reading List

Books

Mead, Lawrence M., *Beyond Entitlement: The Social Obligations of Citizenship,* Free Press, 1985.

Murray, Charles, *Losing Ground: American Social Policy, 1950-1980,* Basic Books, 1984.

Patterson, James T., *America's Struggle Against Poverty, 1900-1980,* Harvard University Press, 1981.

Sheehan, Susan, *A Welfare Mother,* Houghton Mifflin, 1976.

Articles

Duncan, Greg J., and Saul D. Hoffmann, "Welfare Dynamics and the Nature of Need," *Cato Journal,* spring/summer 1986.

Ellwood, David T., and Lawrence H. Summers, "Is Welfare Really the Problem?," *The Public Interest,* spring 1986.

Kaus, Mickey, "The Work Ethic State," *The New Republic,* July 7, 1986.

Kirp, David L., "The California Work/Welfare Scheme," *The Public Interest,* spring 1986.

Lemann, Nicholas, "The Origins of the Underclass," *The Atlantic,* June and July, 1986.

——,"Ghettos: What Has to Be Done," *The Washington Post,* Sept. 8, 1986.

Murray, Charles, "No, Welfare Isn't Really the Problem," *The Public Interest,* summer 1986.

——, "Have the Poor Been 'Losing Ground'?," *Political Science Quarterly,* fall 1985.

——, *"Losing Ground* Two Years Later," *Cato Journal,* spring/summer 1986.

——, "The Two Wars Against Poverty: Economic Growth and the Great Society," *The Public Interest,* fall 1982.

——, "White Welfare Families, 'White Trash,'" *National Review,* March 28, 1986.

Rovner, Julie, "Welfare Reform: The Next Domestic Priority?," *Congressional Quarterly Weekly Report,* Sept. 27, 1986, pp. 2281-2286.

Reports and Studies

Goldman, Barbara, *et al.,* "Final Report on the San Diego Job Search and Work Experience Demonstration," Manpower Demonstration Research Corp., February 1986.

Gueron, Judith M., "Work Initiatives For Welfare Recipients," Manpower Demonstration Research Corp., March 1986.

Graphics: P. 21 photos, Massachusetts Employment and Training Choices program; photo p. 23, CBS Television; photo p. 25, U.S. Dept. of Agriculture; charts p. 26, Richard Pottern; photo p. 28, Chelsea Photographers; logo p. 29, Greater Avenues for Independence; photo p. 30, Ken Heinen; photos pp. 32, 35 and 37, Charles Moseley; photo p. 42, Employee and Training Choices.

HOME HEALTH

Who Cares for the Elderly?

by

Charles J. Moseley

Nov. 21
1 9 8 6

Editor's Note: Since this report was published, the Reagan administration and the 100th Congress have advanced a number of plans to provide increased health benefits to the elderly under Medicare and Medicaid. Following his pledge in the Jan. 27 State of the Union address to submit legislation to Congress "to free the elderly from the fear of catastrophic illness," on Feb. 12 President Reagan endorsed a plan formulated by Secretary of Health and Human Services Otis R. Bowen. *(See p. 62).*

The administration plan would provide Medicare coverage for up to one year of hospital care, as well as cap out-of-pocket Medicare-covered services at $2,000. To cover the added expense, the usual $215 annual Medicare Part B premium would be increased by $60 per year. The administration plan has no provisions for extended community-based health care or nursing home care.

The 100th Congress also has begun to tackle the issue. Four committees held hearings in January. On April 9, the House Ways and Means Health Subcommittee approved a bill to permit Medicare recipients unlimited hospital care and to broaden their coverage to include home and community-based health care and long-term nursing home care in return for higher Medicare insurance payments. Sen. Lloyd Bentsen (D-Texas), chairman of the Senate Finance Committee, had drafted a similar bill.

There is widespread belief in Congress that some legislation to expand health care for the elderly will pass this session, but the extent of new benefits must contend with ever-present budget considerations.

Upsurge in Elderly Home Care

America's elderly population is fast-growing, and thus so are the demands on the nation's health care system. Congress and the Reagan administration have begun to examine home health care as part of a solution to the long-term care requirements of the elderly. Their needs, present and future, are being studies by an administration task force whose report is due by Dec. 15. (See p. 62). The elderly's present needs, combined with new Medicare limits on hospitalization, have caused a boom in home health care services. The boom is attracting for-profit companies to a field once served almost solely by non-profit agencies, creating a multibillion-dollar industry.

It is an industry whose expanded range of products and services holds great promise for many of the 27 million Americans who are 65 and older. By some estimates, one-fifth of the people in this age group must receive home care or else be confined to hospitals or nursing homes. A nationwide survey conducted last year indicates that 72 percent of the general population prefers home care over nursing homes, and that home care has a positive image among 85 percent of the people who are aware of it.[1] The reasons for home care's popularity are financial as well as sentimental.

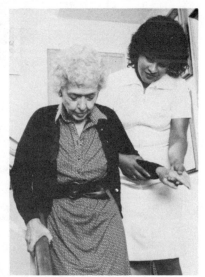

For health planners, government policy makers and health insurance companies, and the patients themselves, there are persuasive reasons for favoring home care over hospital care. In 1985, the average cost of a Medicare-related visit to a home was $53, while per-patient hospital charges averaged $310 a day. The difference would be vastly greater if the patient required use of costly equipment. The American Association of Respiratory Therapy noted in a 1984 report that caring for a ventilator-dependent person at home ran $249,638 less per year than in a hospital.

Recent advances in medical technology have made available to the home many medical procedures and devices that once were confined to institutions. These include intravenous drug

---

[1] The survey was conducted in July 1985 by Market Opinion Research for the National Association for Home Care, Washington, D.C.

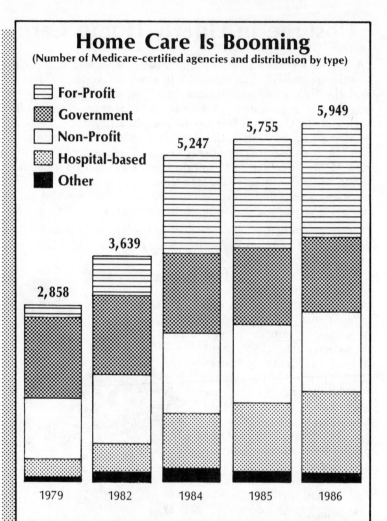

Home Care Is Booming
(Number of Medicare-certified agencies and distribution by type)

- ⊟ For-Profit
- ▨ Government
- ☐ Non-Profit
- ▦ Hospital-based
- ■ Other

2,858 — 1979
3,639 — 1982
5,247 — 1984
5,755 — 1985
5,949 — 1986

Close-Up on Medicare Share

	Home Health Spending (millions)	Annual Increase	Total Visits (millions)	Average Visit Charge
1980	$ 665.7	26.2%	22.6	$ 33
1981	859.5	29.1	26.1	36
1982	1,121.0	30.4	31.2	40
1983	1,426.2	27.2	37.4	43
1984	1,690.9	18.6	40.8	46

SOURCE: *Health Care Financing Administration*

therapy, kidney dialysis, ventilator therapy and direct artificial feeding. Beyond the strictly medical and nursing services, which traditionally have been offered by visiting nurses and therapists, are those that provide cleaning, shopping and cooking for the beleaguered household and assist the patient with such personal functions as feeding, dressing and bathing.

Demographic changes and other social trends suggest that demand for home care services is likely to grow in the future. One factor that is contributing to the increased demand is the population boom among the nation's elderly. Another is the widespread entry into the labor force by women, who historically have been care-givers to the elderly. *(See box, pp. 54-55.)*

Along with the promise that is held forth by this expansion of home care for the elderly — and also for the handicapped of all ages — there is a foretaste of problems ahead. Advocates for the elderly, both individuals and organizations, have expressed to Congress their concern that regulation is inadequate for a growing industry that increasingly is developing a profit motive and attracting health care providers who never before delivered their services to the homes of the ill and infirm.

The House Select Committee on Aging released an August report on home care quality prepared by an American Bar Association (ABA) commission.[2] The committee chairman, Rep. Edward R. Roybal (D-Calif.), called the report "a critical first step in documenting the inadequacy of the present quality assurance system for home care" and told a hearing the decision to release the report was "a statement of the committee's concern."

The hearing followed others conducted by either the committee or its subcommittee on health and long-term care — headed by Rep. Claude Pepper (D-Fla.), now 86 years old, who long has championed causes for the aged. Witnesses testified to a growing need for providing better and less costly health care for the elderly, and cited examples of how care was being denied by the inadequacies of existing provisions and the quirks in government-imposed rules.

Proliferation of For-Profit Health Agencies

The ancestry of the home health care industry can be traced to visiting nurses associations, which arose in the 19th century and today still deliver more health care (about one-third of the total) than any other category of agency.[3] But now there is a

---

[2] The report was drafted by the ABA Commission on Legal Problems of the Elderly, under the chairmanship of John Pickering. The report, titled "The 'Black Box' of Home Care Quality," is Committee Publication No. 99-573, available from the U.S. Government Printing Office, Washington, D.C.

[3] The first home nursing association was founded in Boston in 1886. The first home care program operated by a hospital was established by Montefiore Hospital in New York City in 1947.

greater diversity of providers. In addition to private, non-profit groups, such as the visiting nurses represent, there are government-based agencies and agencies that are operated by hospitals, both for-profit and non-profit. The for-profits, whether run by hospitals or other enterprises, are multiphying. The Health Care Financing Administration (HCFA), which administers Medicare, reports that for-profits accounted for only 6 percent of all home care agencies in 1980 but 32 percent in 1986. *(See box, p. 48.)*

The federal Medicare program does not pay for long-term care either at home or in a nursing home.

Home health care agencies that are certified to receive Medicare reimbursements have more than doubled since 1979, numbering 5,949 in January 1986. The National Association for Home Care estimates that there are more than 10,000 agencies of all kinds providing health care in the home. Although home care still accounts for only 2.4 percent of all Medicare expenditures, it is one of the fastest-growing parts of Medicare, increasing at an average annual rate of 25 percent between 1974 and 1983. Since then the rate has slowed — a fact advocates of the elderly attribute to a stricter intepretation of government-imposed eligibility standards rather than decreased demand. *(See p. 58.)*

The greatest spur to the development of the industry has been the growing cost of health care generally, and especially of institutional care.[4] *(See box, p. 60.)* These costs have made almost any form of outpatient care attractive — and not only to individuals. Insurance companies have come to endorse home care as a way to contain escalating hospital costs. The Blue Cross and Blue Shield Association reported in July 1985 that 90 percent of the Blue Cross/Blue Shield (BC/BS) plans covered home health care. The association said that subscribers in Rhode Island were able to avoid 20,500 days of hospital confinement, at a savings of $6.1 million in 1982-83. Maryland's BC/BS Coordinated Home Care Program reported a $1.2 million sav-

---

[4] For background, see "Health Care: Pressures for Change," *E.R.R.,* 1984 Vol. II, pp. 569-88.

ings in 1982, and a reduction in the average inpatient stay by 8.9 days.

Medicare Overhaul Raises Funding Issue

Home care became not only attractive but, some say, more necessary than ever as a result of a special government effort since 1983 to hold down hospital costs. As directed by Congress that year, Medicare repayment to a hospital was no longer to be based on the actual amount of time patients spent there and the actual medical care they received. It is now determined in advance, according to a schedule of fixed fees based on the type of disease. The system identifies 467 categories of diseases and treatments, called Diagnostic Related Groups (DRGs).

Under this Prospective Payment System, or PPS, the hospital absorbs the loss if the patient is hospitalized longer than the Medicare payment covers. If the patient is discharged sooner, the hospital keeps the difference. With this incentive for quick discharges, hospitals have been accused of sending Medicare patients back to their homes too quickly, making them utterly dependent on some kind of home care — whether provided by government funding, private charity or, most likely, family and friends.

Funding for elderly home care comes from a variety of federal, state and private sources. Medicare, the federal health insurance program for the elderly, provides for short-term home care that follows an acute illness, if certain eligibility criteria are satisfied, but not for long-term care either at the patient's residence or in a nursing home. Medicare paid $1.7 billion for about 41 million home health care visits in 1984.

Medicaid, a joint federal-state program for the poor of all ages, does pay for nursing home care for the indigent.[5] Since 1981, and the establishment of a cost-containment program to reduce public expenditures for nursing home care, Medicaid funds have been available to pay for home care that prevents institutionalization. Medicaid spending for home health care in 1985 was estimated at $1.1 billion.

Some federal funds have been applied to home care since 1974 through Social Security block grants. The Older Americans Act of 1965 also permits some funding for home care, although the funding emphasis has been on nutrition programs. In addition, the Veterans Administration and general revenue funds from the states add to the funding mix for home care. Pennsylvania, for instance, specifies that a portion of income derived from the state lottery goes to programs for the elderly.

---

[5] A 1985 study by Massachusetts Blue Cross/Blue Shield indicated that persons who enter nursing homes paying their own way soon become indigent. Of those surveyed, 63 percent of the unmarried residents of nursing homes had exhausted their assets within 13 weeks and 83 percent had done so within one year.

Quality Control Issues

With the expansion of the home care industry has come increased attention to the issues of quality and regulation. The new pattern of earlier hospital discharges raises two main questions: Who is caring for patients after their release, and how does current care for the elderly compare with that which they previously received in the hospital. Many advocates for the

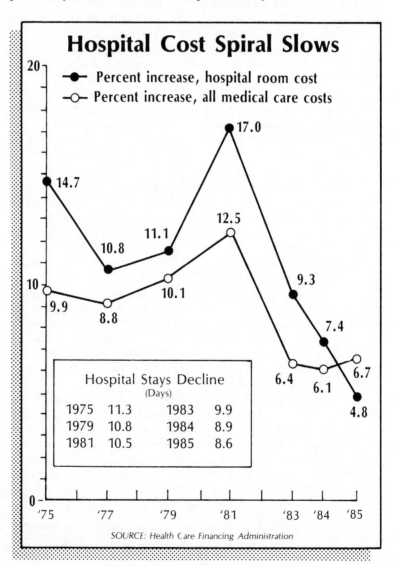

Hospital Cost Spiral Slows

- ●— Percent increase, hospital room cost
- ○— Percent increase, all medical care costs

17.0
14.7
12.5
11.1
10.8
10.1
9.9
8.8
9.3
7.4
6.4
6.1
6.7
4.8

Hospital Stays Decline
(Days)

1975	11.3	1983	9.9
1979	10.8	1984	8.9
1981	10.5	1985	8.6

'75   '77   '79   '81   '83 '84 '85

SOURCE: Health Care Financing Administration

elderly are pressing for regulation — specifically, a standard accreditation process for home care providers, monitoring of the quality of care, and penalties for non-compliance.

As social practice, home health care enjoys an almost reverential reputation, calling to mind family, friends, and charitable societies helping others in time of need. Paid home care workers deliver services in the intimate atmosphere of the patient's own home and participate more completely in the patient's life than those who provide care in an institutional setting.

Advocates for the elderly are pressing for home care regulation, including accreditation and monitoring.

Such normalcy of contact between the patient and the home care worker is key to claims that home medical care is preferable to institutional care. But it is just this aspect of home care that makes the elderly home care patient vulnerable to indifferent service or neglect.

Home care is a service delivered almost invisibly, without some of the ordinary supervisory safeguards that are assumed in other areas of health care. Elderly recipients are, by definition, sick or frail and unable to take care of themselves. Their condition makes them less able than most to resist, report or even perceive mistreatment. And while the home care industry has so far escaped accusations of systematic neglect of patients, isolated incidents of negligence have appeared.

"We hear anecdotal accounts from home care consumers and providers of unreliable and poorly trained aides, of questionable care techniques, and, in some instances, of abuse and neglect," Roybal said in an introduction to the ABA report. "What is most disturbing," he added, "is that we simply do not know how serious or widespread these problems of home care quality are. . . . In these respects, the quality of care in the homes is a 'black box' — a virtual unknown."

Diversity in Accreditation and Licensing

At present there is no comprehensive and consistent regulation of home health care. State licensing is required in 28 states and pending in six others, but requirements and standards of

(continued on p. 56)

Graying of America Means .

Current population trends make clear that the issue of health care will become more pressing. In 1980, an estimated 5.8 million elderly people were disabled to the extent that they needed long-term care. According to projections published by the Population Reference Bureau, this number will more than double to 12.9 million by the year 2020 and reach 18.8 million by 2040.

Most of the non-medical home care — 80 percent by some calculations — needed by the elderly is provided by close family members, and about three-fourths of this care is provided by women. It is usually only when familial care becomes impractical or no family member is available that agencies come on the scene.

But trends in demographics, family structure and the labor force point to a decrease in the care-giving role of family members and thus an increase in the role of home care agencies. A continued increase in the average life span and decrease in the number of children per family will further reduce the number of potential family care-givers in future years.

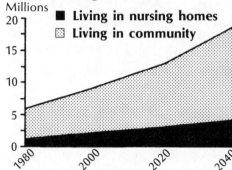

Elderly in Need of Long-Term Care

Millions

■ Living in nursing homes
▨ Living in community

SOURCE: Population Reference Bureau

More Elderly Health Needs

Traditional family structures have changed. The propensity for divorce and remarriage has created more "multiple" families. Although this means a larger family network to care for the elderly, gerontologists and health workers fear this may also weaken family bonds and lessen the sense of obligation.

By far the most important factor eroding the role of the family in providing home health care is the increasing absence of women, to whom most of the care was entrusted. They have left home in ever-growing numbers to take jobs in the work place. Moreover, they are having children later and typically returning to work, thus taking on the dual demands of job and child-rearing that leave virtually no time to care for the family elderly.

Providing such care is likely to be stressful. Research at Duke University's Center on Aging found that one-third of those who care for relatives suffering from Alzheimer's disease used prescription drugs for tension, depression or sleep disorders, as compared with 10 percent of the general population.*

Employers, too, are becoming aware that a worker's health and productivity may suffer from the stresses of caring for the elderly at home. The employee may even use company time to make home care arrangements, consult with doctors or apply for government assistance. Some companies are broadening their employee assistance programs to help workers cope in this situation. Most of these programs supply information about available community resources, but some are exploring changes in company policies and insurance coverage, and even arrangements for offering financial assistance.

*See Linda George and Lisa P. Gwyther in Gerontologist, Vol. 26, No. 3, pp. 253-

(continued from p. 53)

care vary from state to state.[6] Oversight responsibility is usually in the hands of state health departments, which often lack the resources to adequately monitor home care services. The only federal regulatory standard is Medicare certification, which a home care agency needs to obtain Medicare reimbursement.

Self-regulation within the industry appears to be in a transitional stage. Accreditation is provided by the Joint Commission on Accreditation of Hospitals (JCAH) for home care programs provided by hospitals.[7] Almost all hospital-based programs have received accreditation, which includes Medicare certification. The JCAH is currently developing standards to be applied in 1988 for agencies not run by hospitals.

Organizations Concerned with Elderly Home Care

Alzheimer's Disease and Related Disorders Association
Bethesda, Maryland

American Association of Homes for the Aging
Washington, D.C.

American Association of Retired Persons
Washington, D.C.

National Association for Home Care
Washington, D.C.

National Citizens' Coalition for Nursing Home Reform
Washington, D.C.

National Council on the Aging
Washington, D.C.

Also serving as accrediting agencies to the industry are the National League for Nursing, which has accredited about 100 home health and community nursing services, and the National Home Caring Council, which has accredited 140 home-maker and health-aide programs. The for-profit home care agencies generally have not sought accreditations, other than Medicare certification. It has not yet been determined if JCAH accreditation for home care agencies not connected with hospitals will substitute for Medicare certification. If so, these agencies will have an incentive to apply.

The ABA's report noted a scarcity of data on home care quality, criticized the current regulatory mechanisms and recommended uniform standards of accreditation for home care agencies nationwide. The report said this goal would be furthered by extending the Medicare certification requirements to

---

[6] As of August, licensing was required in all states except Alabama, Alaska, Arkansas, Colorado, Indiana, Iowa, Massachusetts, Michigan, Minnesota, Mississippi, Nebraska, Ohio, Oklahoma, South Dakota, Vermont, West Virginia and Wyoming; it was pending in Delaware, Louisiana, Missouri, Pennsylvania, Virginia and the District of Columbia, according to the American Bar Association.

[7] The commission is a private, non-profit, voluntary accrediting body founded by the American Hospital Association, the American Medical Association, the American Dental Association, the American College of Physicians and the American College of Surgeons.

all agencies that receive federal home care funds, even indirectly. It also called for the creation of an ombudsman system to investigate and redress problems that patients encounter, additional monitoring of the quality of home care, and enforcement of standards. Roybal incorporated the report's recommendations into a bill that he plans to reintroduce after the 100th Congress convenes in January.

Horror Stories About Prospective Payments

Congress can also expect to hear more from advocacy groups opposed to the government's Prospective Payment System.

The only federal regulatory standard for home care is Medicare certification, which is needed for Medicare reimbursement.

They argue that this manner of paying Medicare patients' hospital bills promotes the premature termination of hospital care for the elderly. They note that the average stay of a Medicare patient in hospitals using the PPS dropped from 9.3 days in fiscal year 1983 to 7.7 days during the first nine months of 1985. Medicare officials cite those figures to illustrate the system's cost-effectiveness. PPS foes cite them to demonstrate denial of care.

"Our members write heart-wrenching letters about being forcibly discharged from hospitals despite the fact they are too ill to care for themselves," a spokesman for the American Association of Retired Persons (AARP) told Rep. Pepper's subcommittee last March 19. The spokesman, Jack Guildroy of the AARP legislative council, said unmarried older persons still too ill to care for themselves nevertheless were being sent home.

PPS "horror stories" not only have reached Congress but also the publications circulated among health care professionals. Typical of these stories, the magazine *Private Practice* reported that a hospital in New Jersey chose to use the cheapest pacemakers available in patients with the shortest life expectancies — a practice one doctor called "euthanasia by DRG." [8]

Reacting to charges of PPS abuse, the federal government began requiring hospitals to notify Medicare patients of their

---

[8] "Putting PPS in Perspective," Brian Sherman, *Private Practice*, February 1986, p. 35.

right to a review of their case before being discharged, and to plan for any needed follow-up care. In addition, recent legislation requires the Department of Health and Human Services to propose modifications to PPS to allow for differences in case severity and complexity.

Medicare patients discharged from a hospital or who suffer an acute illness that does not require hospitalization do not automatically qualify for home health care. To qualify under current Medicare regulations, beneficiaries must be "homebound" and need part-time skilled nursing care.

AARP and other critics of the system contend that home care is being denied through stringent and even arbitrary application of eligibility rules. They point to HCFA data showing that the denial rate of home care claims more than doubled between the first quarter of 1984 and the first quarter of 1986. There is a further assertion that because more claims are being denied, the providers of home care services are reluctant to accept doubtful cases, in effect acting as a pre-screening agency.

Much of the criticism is not new to Medicare officials. The General Accounting Office, an arm of Congress charged with seeing that laws are applied as lawmakers intend, said five years ago that eligibility rules were unclear, vague and applied inconsistently.[9]

Although HCFA guidelines state that a homebound person normally should not be able to leave home except for infrequent and short trips for non-medical as well as medical purposes, cases have been cited where persons who could not dress, feed or bathe themselves were denied homebound status because they could walk or because they left home to receive kidney dialysis or chemotherapy. As a result, demands are being raised that all home care be covered by Medicare.

Long-Term Care Dilemma

S uch demands confront America's policy makers with a dilemma: Whether to let America's elderly and their families continue to pay enormous bills for long-term care or add to the mounting cost of publicly financed health care.

The debate over home health care has highlighted the much larger problem of gaps in the nation's public health care pro-

---

[9] "Medicare Home Health Services: A Difficult Program to Control," GAO/HRD-81-155, Sept. 25, 1981.

visions for the elderly, especially those having to do with long-term care. Due to differences in coverage and eligibility requirements for Medicare and Medicaid, there is a virtual void in coverage for long-term home care or nursing home care, except for the poor.

A complicating factor is the distinction between long-term home care, which is not covered under Medicare, and short-term home care, which is. In reality, such a distinction is often hard to make. Many elderly patients go through a cycle of relative stability and acute illness within a context of general decline and increasing dependence.

When does the Medicare-covered care end and the uncovered long-term custodial care begin? Although the distinction is crucial to government payment, it is a constant source of frustration to the elderly and to those providing the care. The majority of Americans are unaware of this distinction or gaps in coverage until they are forced to seek care for a family member or for themselves. A 1984 poll by the Gallup Organization Inc. found that 79 percent of the respondents erroneously believed that all nursing home care was covered under Medicare. In fact, Medicare only pays for a tiny fraction of the elderly's nursing home bill. Medicaid pays about half of the total cost, and consumers foot practically all of the rest of the bill out of pocket.

The long-term care problem is illustrated by the current shortage of nursing home beds. Compared with a 60 percent occupancy rate for the nation's hospital beds, nursing homes are currently operating at 95 percent capacity, according to the American Health Care Association. In some areas of the country, as reported last May by the Senate Special Committee on Aging, the bed shortage in nursing homes is so great that relatives are often forced to offer "additional payments" to place a family member in one of the homes.

More nursing home beds will be needed as the over-85 population grows. This age group, the most likely to need nursing home care, is expected to grow faster than any other, according to the Census Bureau. In 1980, 10 percent of the elderly were over 85, but by 2040 that figure will be almost 20 percent.

However, many state governments are trying to keep their Medicaid budgets stable. One means to do this is by keeping a tight control on the number of nursing home beds. Kentucky, Minnesota, Mississippi, North Carolina, Virginia and Wisconsin, for example, have placed a moratorium on new nursing home beds. Others are enacting stricter standards for certifying construction of new facilities.

Increasingly, the lack of publicly funded long-term care for the elderly is sparking a wide-scale policy debate. Some congres-

Nursing Home Bills Are on the Rise

Year	Billions $
1970	$4.7
'71	$5.6
'72	$6.5
'73	$7.2
'74	$8.5
'75	$10.1
'76	$11.3
'77	$13.0
'78	$15.1
'79	$17.4
'80	$20.4
'81	$23.9
'82	$26.9
'83	$29.4
'84	$32.0
'85	$35.2

Billions $ 5 10 15 20 25 30 35

SOURCE: Health Care Financing Administration

Who Pays?

	1985 Share
Consumer out of pocket	51.4%
Medicaid	41.8
Medicare	1.7
Private insurance	0.8
All other sources	4.3

SOURCE: Health Care Financing Administration

sional plans propose expanding public programs, while the Reagan administration is expected soon to propose greater involvement by the private sector. The issue of cost figures prominently in this debate. Expanding Medicare would imply big increases in public funding, a major drawback in today's deficit-conscious political arena. But questions remain as to whether private-sector solutions would be affordable to the elderly.

As the debate over long-term care unfolds, the role of home care in a long-term care system is being evaluated in terms of whether it would reduce institutional care and how costly it would be. In recent experimental programs, such as the New York City Home Care Project and the San Diego Long-Term Care Project, home health care did not produce overall cost savings.

Long-term home care was added to Medicaid in 1981 as an experiment in reducing costs. Under the Medicaid Home- and Community-Based Waiver Program, states were allowed to give long-term home care services to those poor who would otherwise need institutional care. While all agree that these programs, which have been approved in 46 states, have delivered needed services to chronically ill elderly, there is little evidence that they have slowed the rate of institutionalization or reduced total costs.[10] Because families usually resist putting a member in a nursing home as long as they can, many analysts see long-term home care as an expansion of services to the elderly and not a replacement for nursing home care.

However, Brookings Institution analyst Raymond J. Hanley argues that studies of expanded home health care services have shown that at-home elderly are happier and more satisfied with their care. Said Hanley: "Life significance goes up when the elderly are able to stay at home, but OMB [the Office of Management and Budget] is more interested in cost-efficiency."

Proposals to Expand or Replace Medicare

Long-term home care coverage was part of a proposed expansion of the Medicare system presented last summer to the House Select Committee on Aging.[11] Dr. David Blumenthal, author of a study by Harvard University's Center for Health Policy and Management, noted that America's elderly now pay about the same proportion of their annual income (15 percent) as they did before the introduction of Medicare two decades ago.

The report recommended that Medicare coverage be extended and include home health care and nursing home care.

---

[10] Alaska, Arizona, Arkansas and Wyoming do not participate in the waiver program.
[11] "The Future of Medicare," *New England Journal of Medicine*, March 13, 1986.

Elderly patients would be expected to pay 80 percent of their Social Security benefits for "room and board" if they were in a nursing home, or the equivalent of one month's home care charge if they received home care services.

The report estimated that such an extension of coverage would add $50 billion annually to the overall cost of the program. The study pointed out, however, that the net increase in government funding would be only $15 billion, because Medicaid expenditures for long-term care would decrease by $35 billion. Because of the size of the added expenditures, the study recommended that long-term care be phased in over 10 years, beginning in 1990.

Rep. Roybal, who favors expanding Medicare, is planning to introduce legislation to establish a comprehensive health insurance plan, available to Americans of all ages, as a replacement for Medicare and Medicaid. His plan would cover both home health care and nursing home care. Other plans for dealing with long-term care have surfaced. In one, Pepper has joined Sen. Jim Sasser (D-Tenn.) in proposing legislation to give Medicare recipients the option of receiving nursing home or long-term home care for payment of a flat annual fee.

In contrast to the congressional plans favoring expanding Medicare to provide long-term care, an administration task force set up by Health and Human Services Secretary Otis R. Bowen has focused on the private sector.[12] The group has completed its work and is expected to deliver its findings to the White House in December. Those findings reportedly will emphasize the cost factors of long-term care and recommend that such care should be financed by the private sector, not the public sector.

Debate Over Private-Sector Options

Two private-sector approaches already have attracted attention. One comes from large private insurance companies, in the form of narrowly tailored insurance policies that provide long-term health care for the elderly.[13] These relatively new policies are one of the fastest-selling forms of insurance on the market. As of this year, an estimated 200,000 Americans have bought this insurance, which covers long nursing home stays and home care services for disabled elderly persons. According to the American Health Care Association, the number of policyholders could double to 400,000 next year.

---

[12] The task force, headed by James Bailoz, vice chairman of Drexell Burnham Lambert, includes representatives from Congress and the insurance industry, health care providers and advocates for the elderly.

[13] These insurance plans are discussed in Steven Greenhouse, "Health Insurance for Elderly: A New Option," *The Wall Street Journal*, Oct. 13, 1986.

The new policies, typically offered to people in their 50s to early 80s, are usually renewable for life. They generally pay a fixed amount in benefits — between $10 and $120 — for each day in a nursing home for a period of time ranging from two to six years. Some of the policies also cover home care services for several months, often at a rate of about half the daily nursing home benefit. Most policies do not cover pre-existing conditions. Premiums range from $250 to $2,500 a year.

From the standpoint of home care, the new insurance policies are far less than ideal. Some provide home care services only if preceded by hospital care for the same illness or accident, raising the same eligibility problems as Medicare. Some limit coverage to skilled nursing care. Policies that do provide comprehensive home care coverage are far costlier.

Moreover, the larger question of whether private insurance can serve the long-term care needs of the less-affluent elderly remains open. "Policy studies ... clearly demonstrate that private long-term care insurance won't address the need. The well-off will be able to afford coverage but most people won't be able to afford to protect themselves against risk," said Nancy Smith, an aide to the House Aging Committee.

The other private-sector approach to the problem, still on the drawing board, was supported by Bowen in an article written before he became head of HHS.[14] It would establish health care savings accounts, along the lines of individual retirement accounts (IRAs), in which middle-aged workers would receive tax breaks for investing for their health care in later years. Workers would be allowed to contribute an amount equal to that paid by them and their employers in Medicare payroll taxes, and would receive a tax credit of 60 percent of that amount.

Detractors of the idea have argued that no matter how much sense it makes on paper, the idea of nursing home care is so intrinsically unappealing that most people will not invest their money voluntarily in any fund that reminds them of such an unpleasant prospect.

However the debate over long-term health care turns out, it almost certainly will be a subject for heated partisan debate in Washington. With Democrats now controlling both houses of Congress, they can be expected to take a hard look at the private-sector solution the administration is expected to unveil soon. A key arena for the battle as it shapes up in Congress will be the House Select Committee on Aging, which plans to hold extensive hearings. "Last year was the 'year of quality' in home care," said Smith. "Next year we plan to focus on the need for long-term care."

---

[14] *Federation of American Hospitals Review*, November/December 1985.

Recommended Reading List

Articles

Doty, P., K. Liu, and J. Wiener, "An Overview of Long-Term Care," *Health Care Financing Review*, Vol. 6, No. 3, spring 1985.

Friedman, Dana E., "Eldercare: The Employee Benefit of the 1990s?," *Across the Board* (published by The Conference Board), Vol. 23, No. 6, June 1986.

Koren, Mary Jane, "Home Care — Who Cares?" *The New England Journal of Medicine*, Vol. 314, No. 14, April 3, 1986.

Rovner, Julie, "Long-Term Care: The True 'Catastrophe'?" *Congressional Quarterly*, May, 31, 1986, pp. 1227-31.

Weissert, William G., "The Cost-Effectiveness Trap," *Generations*, summer 1985.

Reports

"The 'Black Box' of Home Care Quality," American Bar Association Commission on Legal Problems of the Elderly, presented August 1986 to the House Select Committee on Aging, U.S. Government Printing Office, 1986.

Day, Alice T., "Who Cares? Demographic Trends Challenge Family Care for the Elderly," Population Reference Bureau Inc., 1985.

Leader, Shelah, "Home Health Benefits Under Medicare," Public Policy Institute of the American Association of Retired Persons, September 1986.

Graphics: Photo p. 47, National Medical Enterprises Inc.; charts pp. 48 and 52, Jack Auldridge; photos pp. 53 and 57, Caring Magazine; charts pp. 54, 56 and 60, Robert Redding; photo p. 55, Mark Kaminsky.

Blueprints for
National Service

by Robert K. Landers

Oct. 31
1 9 8 6

What Can Be Done For the Country?

Kennedy

"*Now the trumpet summons us again.*" On an icy cold January day in 1961, President Kennedy urged his fellow Americans: "Ask not what your country can do for you — ask what you can do for your country." Within six weeks of his Inaugural Address, the new president signed an executive order establishing the Peace Corps. There was in America, Kennedy said on that occasion, "an immense reservoir" of men and women eager "to sacrifice their energies and time and toil to the cause of world peace and human progress." Life in the Peace Corps would not be easy, he said, but it would be "rich and satisfying." Thousands of young Americans agreed, and within six months the first groups of trained volunteers — teachers and road surveyors — were bound for Africa.

The Peace Corps and Volunteers in Service to America (VISTA), a domestic version established in 1964 that also re-

A Peace Corps volunteer threshing rice in Niger.

cruited, in the main, young college graduates as volunteers, represented one form of American idealism. But it was soon overshadowed by another — the Vietnam War. As a result of that unhappy experience, a disillusioned America has seemed little inclined to heed any sonorous calls to national sacrifice and service. Military conscription was brought to an end in 1973. During President Reagan's first term, his administration repeatedly, if unsuccessfully, tried to bring to an end the VISTA program, too. Even the Peace Corps had only 6,264 volunteers in 1985—two-fifths the number in 1966. To many in the early 1980s, America and its youth seemed preoccupied with material wealth and private gain.[1]

But now there are signs that American idealism may be stirring again. On college campuses, there seems to be new interest in volunteer community service. Just a year ago, 75 university presidents announced the formation of a coalition to encourage students to take part in such service. Brown University President Howard Swearer said there were indications that "there are more students willing to take advantage of public service opportunities if they are presented with opportunities to do so." [2] Brown offered fellowships to students who spent a year in public service; by the university's 1985 estimate, a fourth of its undergraduates were involved in community service.

Among the nation's leaders, Democratic politicians with their eyes on the 1988 presidential election — including Sen. Gary Hart of Colorado and former Virginia Gov. Charles S. Robb — have begun to deploy the rhetoric of challenge and sacrifice. They have called for the creation of a system of national service, one that would summon American youths to do socially useful work, such as preserving the environment, caring for the elderly and assisting the poor.

The idea of national service is not a new one. In the first decade of this century, American philosopher William James proposed creating a "moral equivalent of war" in which there would be "a conscription of the whole youthful population to form for a certain number of years a part of the army enlisted against *Nature," (See box, opposite page.)* The notion has since taken many forms and attracted many American idealists, including several presidents.

But for a variety of reasons, not least the sheer scope and cost of any genuinely national system of service, the idea has only been translated into reality to a very limited extent. The New Deal's Civilian Conservation Corps (CCC), for instance, over the nine years of its existence sent an average of fewer than 350,000 unemployed young men a year into the woods to do conserva-

---

[1] See "Student Politics 1980s Style," *E.R.R.*, 1986 Vol. II, pp. 609-28.
[2] Quoted in *The New York Times*, Oct. 17, 1985.

James

A Pacifist's Vision: 'Moral Equivalent of War'

The idea of national service is usually tracked back to the American philosopher and psychologist William James (1842-1910). James, a pacifist, was appalled by the Spanish-American War of 1898 and what he saw as the rise of "an 'imperialist' party" that commanded "all the crude and barbaric patriotism of the country." In a Stanford University speech in 1906, he spoke of the need for a "moral equivalent of war." *

History, he said, was "a bath of blood," and war "the gory nurse that trained societies to cohesiveness." Yet the martial virtues were "absolute and permanent human goods." Peace would not reign until it became war's equal at sustaining those values.

James proposed, as a substitute for military conscription, "a conscription of the whole youthful population to form for a certain number of years a part of the army enlisted against *Nature*." The utopian proposal would have applied only to young men, would have been compulsory, and would have been a substitute for — not a complement to — military service. Indeed, the very purpose of organizing a "moral equivalent of war" was so that mankind could do away with war.

Elaborating on the army's purpose, James said: "To coal and iron mines, to freight trains, to fishing fleets in December, to dish-washing, clothes-washing, and window-washing, to road-building and tunnel-making, to foundries and stoke-holes, and to the frames of sky-scrapers, would our gilded youths be drafted off, according to their choice, to get the childishness knocked out of them, and to come back into society with healthier sympathies and soberer ideas."

* *Gay Wilson Allen in* William James *(1967), p. 389; and "The Moral Equivalent of War," in Bruce W. Wilshire, ed.,* William James: The Essential Writings *(paper, 1984), pp. 349-361.*

tion work. The Peace Corps, since its founding in 1961, has sent more than 120,000 Americans to work in 94 countries, but the most volunteers it had in any one year was 15,556. *(See box, p. 72.)* The modest VISTA program, which dispatched volunteers to work among the American poor in rural Appalachia, in city slums, and on Indian reservations, never had more than 5,000 volunteers annually, even at its height.

And yet, the idea of national service has continued to attract advocates and interest. One reason is that, despite the intent of pacifist James and despite the desires of many modern proponents, it has often been linked with military conscription. National service is seen by some as a way of making the draft more acceptable and less unfair. Consequently, when revival of the draft comes up for discussion, so, often, does national service.

For the most part, however, the idea has continued to be attractive — with or without a military aspect — as a way to reawaken patriotism, make society more cohesive, infuse America's youth with a sense of common purpose, uplift the poor, and spiritually enrich the affluent.

Inspirational Dream, Logistical Headache

Some prominent Democratic politicians are among the most enthusiastic proponents of the idea of national service:

● Hart in February 1985 unveiled "a vision of a new idealism based upon true patriotism." The vision included a system of national service, civilian and military, for young Americans, challenging them, he said, "to use their energies, not only for their own purposes and interests, but for the needs and interests of our nation as well." He proposed establishing a commission to study whether national service should be voluntary or compulsory, how it would affect the all-volunteer Army, and other pertinent matters.

● Robb in September of this year called for "some form of universal national service" in a speech to the National Conference of Editorial Writers in Charleston, S.C. "I realize that there are formidable administrative problems involved," he said, "but I don't think it's too much to ask that each young American render his or her country a period of military or civilian service."

● The Robb-chaired Democratic Leadership Council — in a report in September over the signatures of Sens. Sam Nunn of Georgia and Albert Gore Jr. of Tennessee and Rep. Les Aspin of Wisconsin — called for an examination of the possibility of establishing a system of national service, both civilian and military. The council said that over the next 10 years the demographic pool from which military recruits are drawn will shrink, making it difficult to maintain the quality or size of the all-volunteer military "without driving up its already considerable cost." National service, it said, "could bolster our national strength and foster a new spirit of citizenship and patriotism." [3]

● The Coalition for a Democratic Majority's Task Force on Foreign Policy and Defense — chaired by Rep. Dave McCurdy of Oklahoma and counting Robb, Aspin and Boston University President John Silber among its members — this month called for "a broad and voluntary program of national service," civilian

Former Virginia Gov. Charles S. Robb and Sen. Gary Hart are among Democratic proponents of national service.

or military, for America's youth. "By giving the duties of citizenship a central place in the national service debate," the coalition said, "military and civilian service can be presented as complementary rather than opposed concepts. . . ." Although it should be voluntary, the coalition said, the program could attract "a large proportion of eligible young people." The incentive for participation would be educational assistance.

The American public, too, seems to like the idea of national service. In a 1983 poll by the Gallup Organization Inc., 65 percent of the public — and 58 percent of those aged 18-24 — favored requiring one year of national service from all young men and women.

By certain American scholars, the concept is viewed as vital to America. Northwestern University sociologist Charles C. Moskos in 1981 proposed linking federal aid for higher education to a voluntary national service system that would include military-reserve duty or civilian work. "The grand design," he wrote, "is that the ideal of citizenship obligation ought to become part of growing up in America." [4] And University of Chicago sociologist Morris Janowitz argued in a 1984 book that it was necessary to restore the balance between citizenship's rights and obligations, and to rebuild patriotism in modern form.[5]

---

[3] "Defending America: Building a New Foundation for National Strength," Democratic Leadership Council, September 1986, p. 20.

[4] Charles C. Moskos, "Making the All-Volunteer Force Work: A National Service Approach," *Foreign Affairs*, fall 1981, p. 34.

[5] Morris Janowitz, *The Reconstruction of Patriotism: Education for Civic Consciousness* (paper, 1985 [1984]), p. 194.

Big Ideas, Small Realities

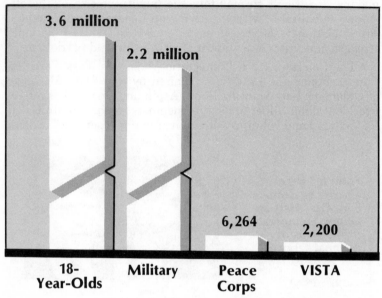

A national service made up of all 18-year-olds would be more than half again as large as today's active-duty military and would dwarf the Peace Corps and Volunteers in Service to America (VISTA). Data are for 1985.

SOURCES: Census Bureau, Defense Department, Peace Corps, VISTA

The volunteer spirit, as reflected here in Peace Corps enrollment, may be on the rebound.

SOURCE: Peace Corps

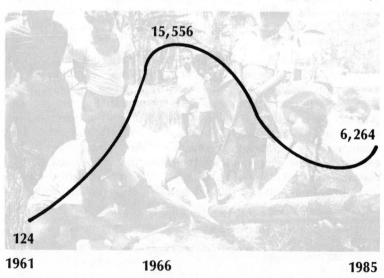

The idea of national service received close scrutiny this year in a study commissioned by the Ford Foundation and conducted by former Carter administration officials Richard Danzig and Peter Szanton. "Military veterans, Peace Corps alumni, and, ironically, immigrants," they wrote, "are now virtually the only Americans who experience a sense of citizenship earned rather than simply received. As a result, they often value themselves and their country more highly. Forms of national service that required sacrifice, intensive effort, or some risk might offer that sense to all." [6]

But establishing a workable system of national service would not be easy. If the system were voluntary, participation might well be insufficient to make the service truly national or to produce a new spirit of patriotism. If the system were compulsory, the challenge of making it work would be formidable indeed. About 4 million Americans turn 18 every year, and alongside that number, the 6,000 or so volunteers in the Peace Corps and the even fewer in VISTA shrink into numerical insignificance.

"With national service that attempts to be truly national in scope," said Danzig in an interview, "you're talking about a bigger adventure than this society's ever undertaken." The experience in the Vietnam War, for instance, "doesn't begin to talk about the numbers of people" that would be involved. In the entire U.S. active-duty military, Danzig noted, there are about 2.1 million people. "And now we're talking about taking in [for national service] 4 million people per year, every year, year after year. I don't think that there's much probability that society will jump into that pool without going step by step, inch by inch."

Pilot Projects: '60s and '30s Style

A mong the modern national leaders who have entertained the notion of national service was President Johnson. In 1965, speaking at the University of Kentucky, he said he intended to "continue to search for new ways" for every young American to "have the opportunity — and feel the obligation — to give at least a few years of his or her life to the service of others in the nation and in the world." Johnson's search finally came to naught, but at the Peace Corps and the Office of Economic

---

[6] Richard Danzig and Peter Szanton, *National Service: What Would It Mean?* (1986), p. 277. Danzig, a lawyer, was principal deputy assistant defense secretary for manpower and logistics during the Carter administration. Szanton, who heads a consulting firm, was an associate director of the Office of Management and Budget.

Opportunity, some officials in his administration were working, as former Associate Peace Corps Director Harris Wofford has recounted, "to propose steps that would lead toward such universal voluntary service by young Americans." [7] National service, they thought, would supply the War on Poverty with the troops it really needed: First tens of thousands, then hundreds of thousands, and then a million a year.

Johnson had tapped Peace Corps Director R. Sargent Shriver to also head the anti-poverty crusade. Shriver harked back to James for his vision. "To eliminate poverty at home, and to achieve peace in the world," Shriver wrote, "we need the total commitment, the large-scale mobilization, the institutional invention, the unprecedented release of human energy, and the focusing of intellect which have happened in our society only in war. We need what William James called 'the moral equivalent of war.' " [8]

As he directed the anti-poverty war, Shriver hoped that if Peace Corps and VISTA volunteers (most of them affluent and white) joined with the volunteers of the Job Corps (most of them poor and black), they could form "a giant pincers movement converging in the great center, which is smug and self-satisfied and complacent." In reality, however, Wofford has noted, "there was nothing bringing them together." [9]

The large-scale national service program that Wofford and his colleagues wanted would have corrected that defect. It would have brought together "a cross section of young people, from city, suburb, small town, and farm, college-bound and those stopping with high school, rich and poor, black and white. The experience of such diverse young people living and working together would be different from anything most of them would have ever known. For the rich, it should enrich their lives, in ways Peace Corps service had done for most volunteers. For some of the poorest youth, participation in national service could save lives. It would keep them from sinking into the ranks of the unemployed right away after leaving school. After a year or two of challenging and disciplined service, many of them should emerge with the hope, ambition, and sense of confidence necessary to cope in a difficult and demanding society." [10]

Wofford and the others were elated when a leader of what James would have considered "the war party" — Defense Secretary Robert S. McNamara — took up the idea of national

---

[7] Harris Wofford, *Of Kennedys and Kings: Making Sense of the Sixties* (1980), p. 312.
[8] R. Sargent Shriver, *Point of the Lance* (1964), pp. 6-7.
[9] Wofford, *op. cit.*, p. 312. Shriver's remark is quoted by Wofford on p. 299.
[10] *Ibid.*, p. 312.

service. In a 1966 speech, McNamara suggested that the inequity of having only "a minority of eligible young men" drafted into the military could begin to be rectified by "asking every young person in the United States to give two years of service to his country — whether in one of the military services, in the Peace Corps or in some other volunteer developmental work at home or abroad." But the White House quickly threw cold water on the suggestion and eventually, in Wofford's words, "made it clear that because of the mounting costs of the conflict in Vietnam there would be no money for any such large new venture." [11]

VISTA in Appalachia

In Search of a Contemporary Model

Although it thus came to nothing in the '60s, the idea of universal national service for youths of high school or college age still remains alive in the '80s. According to Danzig and Szanton, there are almost 3.5 million full-time jobs of social value — in education, health, child care, environment, and other fields — that people in national service in the late 1980s or early '90s could do. "People who oppose national service on a theory of, well, there isn't enough work for 4 million 18-year-olds, are just wrong," Danzig said.

But the fact that the work is there does not mean that national service would fulfill in the best possible way every purpose proclaimed by advocates. For, Danzig said, the youths would not be getting "especially good employment training," and national service would not be an "especially cheap" way of getting the work done.

Most American high school students already have had experience working for pay outside the home, Danzig and Szanton observed. National service jobs would not necessarily provide better work experience, and most such jobs would not naturally lead to private-sector jobs. "Well-run service programs," Danzig

[11] *Ibid.*, pp. 315-16.

and Szanton wrote, "would provide to some disadvantaged participants socialization to the demands of the workplace, including discipline, teamwork, and punctuality." But, they added, the question is: "Would the disadvantaged be better served by such programs or by job training that made no pretense of service? The answer is unclear, but we think the evidence favors the latter hypothesis." [12]

National service also would not be inexpensive. "As a practical matter," Danzig said, "the costs of running a national service system, of dealing with the turbulence and turnover if you had people serve for just a year, getting them into the right assignments, screening them, telling them what to do, having supervisors discipline them, and all that sort of stuff, the costs of that, plus the costs of paying these people a subsistence wage, make that work really not cheaper than going out and hiring a minimum-wage worker in the market."

However, Danzig argued, if national service is to be done mainly "for what we think is the most valid reason, which is to educate the participants in national service to what it's like to serve people, and broaden their horizons and so on, [then] yes, you could find enough work there for them to do that would be useful work to do."

Various systems to get American youth to do such work have been conjured up over the years. One of these is a federally subsidized program that would let states require 240 hours of unpaid service from high school seniors as a prerequisite for graduation. Such a program, however, for better or worse, would not reach youths who drop out of high school before their senior year. An even more selective proposal was made by conservative writer William F. Buckley Jr. in 1973. He proposed that the 10 "top-rated" private colleges and universities in the country adopt an admissions requirement that entering freshmen must have spent a year helping to care for the elderly in nursing homes, or a year in some other form of public service.[13] College presidents recently have set about encouraging students to do volunteer service, but they have not gone that far.

For many middle- and upper-class youths, there seems little doubt that national service might prove rewarding. Mimi Mager, executive director of Friends of VISTA,[14] noted that the Peace Corps or VISTA gave many volunteers "their first expo-

---

[12] Danzig and Szanton, *op. cit.*, pp. 272-73.
[13] See William F. Buckley Jr., *Four Reforms: A Guide for the Seventies* (1973), pp. 14-18.
[14] Friends of VISTA, co-chaired by Shriver and former Michigan Gov. George W. Romney, is a Washington-based organization devoted to supporting the VISTA program. Founded in early 1980, Friends of VISTA has been in the unusual position during the Reagan administration of being more in favor of the program than are the people running it. Congress this month reauthorized VISTA for three years and also created a VISTA literacy corps to help public and non-profit agencies combat illiteracy.

sure to poverty and ... to real problems that disadvantaged people face, and for many of them, it really changed their life." One former volunteer who was born to great wealth is Sen. John D. Rockefeller IV, D-W.Va. He worked with the Peace Corps in "its very early days," then briefly with the State Department, and then in 1964 moved to West Virginia as a VISTA volunteer in the Action for Appalachian Youth program. The experience, he told a House subcommittee in 1985, "totally changed" his life and made him decide to go into public service.

As he looked back on VISTA, Rockefeller said, "I return to this question that runs through my head all the time. If we have these problems in our country, whose job is it to worry about them? ... I think the answer is that it is the job of all of us. Somehow VISTA made it real to many young Americans, that it was part of their responsibility, 'their' being the whole society. The whole society had to look out for the whole society and care for the whole society." That experience, he said, was "deeply fulfilling." [15]

The question, however, is how great the rewards are to society from having privileged youths thus psychologically fulfilled at public expense? Mager said that many Peace Corps and VISTA alumni "have committed ... their careers to social service programs. But I think even if they've gone on to be president of [a] corporation or to work for [a] Wall Street firm, there's something there that stays. There's that sensitivity to problems that people have who are hungry or illiterate...." But according to Danzig and Szanton, "there is no evidence that Peace Corps volunteers contribute more to U.S. public life after their service than they would have done without their service." Several studies of returned Peace Corps volunteers, the authors noted, indicated that the returned volunteers participated less in volunteer or altruistic organizations than did their peers who had declined to join the Peace Corps.[16]

"Taken without regard to the value of the Peace Corps to U.S. foreign policy or to recipients of services," Danzig and Szanton wrote, "we do not believe that the effects on the participants justify much of that program's cost of more than $20,000 annually per volunteer." Commented Mager: "I think if you look at it as ... sort of an experiment, one could certainly say, 'This is a pretty expensive experiment. Maybe we should just see what happens if these kids sort of wing it on their own.' But I think that if you look at any of the [volunteer service] programs

---

[15] Testimony before the House Education and Labor Committee's Subcommittee on Select Education, June 18, 1985.

[16] Danzig and Szanton, *op. cit.*, pp. 160, 202. The studies, the authors observed, are "at most, suggestive. They do not address what seems to us to be the plausible hypothesis that the comparative value of service experience is not necessarily great in the short term but rises with time."

... the impact on the individual as well as the impact on the community and therefore on society is great."

New Deal Program Gave Work to Jobless

In evaluating the worth of national service, Danzig and Szanton argued, the costs — to both participants and society — of the opportunities forgone by the individuals must be taken into account. Those costs vary enormously. Danzig and Szanton cite, as an example, the history of the Civilian Conservation Corps (CCC), the New Deal program that sent unemployed youths into the woods to do conservation work.

The CCC was established soon after President Roosevelt took office in 1933; by the end of July of that year, more than 300,000 young men were enrolled and at work. "They discharged a thousand conservation tasks which had gone too long unperformed," historian Arthur M. Schlesinger Jr. has recounted.[17] But, he wrote, they did more "than reclaim and develop natural resources. They reclaimed and developed themselves. They came from large cities and from small towns, from slum street corners and from hobo jungles, from the roads and the rails and from nowhere.... Their muscles hardened, their bodies filled out, their self-respect returned. They learned trades; more important, they learned about America, and they learned about other Americans."

More than 2.5 million young men passed through the CCC camps in the nine years of its existence; the top enrollment was more than 500,000 in 1935. The CCC, wrote Schlesinger, was "one of the most fortunate of New Deal inventions.... For the President, who had mused about the possibility of setting up some form of universal service for youth since the First World War, CCC remained particularly close to his heart." National service advocates Donald J. Eberly and Michael W. Sherraden have declared: "Of all the public service programs in the United States to date, the CCC most nearly approximated the moral equivalent described by William James." [18]

The history of the CCC, Danzig and Szanton wrote, indicates how extensively "opportunity costs" vary over time. At first, the CCC "offered income and a chance to be useful when both such opportunities were in short supply." But as the Depression receded and ordinary jobs became more available, the CCC shifted its focus to education and training — "and it was notably less popular." Then the manpower needs of World War II made such civilian national service largely irrelevant and the program was abandoned. Despite the success of the CCC, it was

---

[17] See Arthur M. Schlesinger Jr., *The Coming of the New Deal* (1958), pp. 337-40.
[18] Donald J. Eberly and Michael W. Sherraden, "National Service Precedents in the United States," in Sherraden and Eberly, *National Service: Social, Economic and Military Impacts* (1982), p. 42.

not resumed when the war was over and the economy was booming. This history, Danzig and Szanton concluded, "suggests that a large-scale national service program would likely be enacted only when alternative economic and educational opportunities were so poor and military manpower demands so low as to leave a large portion of the population, and especially of youth, without an obviously useful occupation." [19]

The Military Connection: Pro and Con

Although most advocates of national service are concerned mainly with civilian service, others are at least equally concerned with strengthening the military. They want to draw into its ranks more educated, middle-class youths and so make the force better qualified and more representative of the larger society. Some advocates think this could be accomplished on a voluntary basis, by offering educational benefits as an inducement. But others think compulsion would be necessary and favor a revival of the draft. As part of a system of national service, a draft might be made fairer than it would otherwise be and might be brought into being more easily. Whether national service would actually strengthen the military, however, is at least open

[19] Danzig and Szanton, *op. cit.*, pp. 275-76.

A CCC work crew sawing timber in Washington state.

to argument, for the civilian and military components would to some extent be competing for the same youths.

In the late 1970s, concerns about the adequacy of the all-volunteer military force prompted talk of the need to return to a draft and of creating a system of national service with a military component. Despite the talk, however, there was no return to the draft and no serious move toward national service. But the experience illustrated how strong the link seems to be between national service and military conscription. Perceived problems with military manpower, Danzig observed, have "an imperative to being cured that is stronger than the ideological imperative in favor of national service by a big margin."

After the United States abandoned conscription in 1973, experts concerned about military manpower began to worry about the efficacy of a strictly volunteer force. Could a sufficient number of qualified volunteers be recruited and retained? The doubts became strongest in the late '70s, especially when the anticipated decline over the 1980s in qualified and available 18-year-old males was contemplated. In 1977-80, more than a fourth of new military recruits — and more than two-fifths of the Army's new male recruits — scored in the lowest category on the Armed Forces Qualification Test.

Volunteer Army Sparks Manpower Debate

An improvement in the nation's economy was among the factors responsible for the difficulties in recruiting and retaining qualified volunteers, according to Martin Binkin, a senior fellow at The Brookings Institution. Other factors were a failure to keep military pay competitive with civilian pay; a reduction in educational benefits for members of the armed forces, and a failure to keep recruiting and advertising budgets even with inflation. Also, Binkin has written, the military's public image had been tarnished by the 1979 failed rescue mission in Iran and the dubious success in the 1975 *Mayaguez* incident, in which 38 lives were lost in rescuing a U.S. merchant ship and its crew of 39.[20]

Besides the strong doubts about the all-volunteer force's quality in the late '70s, there were also concerns that it was not representative, in its class or racial composition, of the larger society and that that was unfair. However, a simple return to conscription did not seem feasible, given the likely public resistance. National service was a proposed solution. "One of the reasons this whole national service debate came up in the late '70s," Binkin said in an interview, "was that it was kind of going to be the sugar coating for selective service."

---

[20] Martin Binkin, *America's Volunteer Military: Progress and Prospects* (1984), p. 1.

Manpower: How Less Means More

Because the youth population is shrinking, the all-volunteer military has to get a larger share of the pool of available 18-year-olds.

Proportion of Qualified and Available Males Required for Military Service

Thousands unless otherwise indicated

	Annual average		
	1981-83	1984-88	1991-95
Total 18-year-old males	**2,049**	**1,827**	**1,637**
Minus: Nonavailable	626	552	489
Institutionalized	31	27	25
College enrollees less first- or second-year dropouts	595	525	464
Minus: Unqualified	576	526	461
Mental	363	337	291
Physical or moral	213	189	170
Equals: Qualified and available male pool	**847**	**749**	**687**
Total male recruit requirements	**354**	**376**	**376**
Active forces	270	278	278
Reserve forces	84	98	98
Percent of pool required	**42**	**50**	**55**

SOURCE: "America's Volunteer Military"

Rep. Paul N. McCloskey, R-Calif., in 1979 put forward one plan for a national service. His proposal would have given 18-year-old men and women the choice of volunteering for two years of military service, which would entitle them to educational benefits; or for six months of active duty followed by five-and-a-half years in the reserves; or for one year of civilian service; or for none of the above. Youths who selected the last option would then have been subject to a military draft lottery and liable for six years to be conscripted for a term of two years of active duty and four years in the reserves, with reduced educational benefits. Binkin — who regards national service as appealing in the abstract but almost always deficient in the actuality — said McCloskey's plan seemed "fairly reasonable." But it, like one proposed by Rep. John J. Cavanaugh, D-Neb., got nowhere. If, as turned out to be the case, there was not to be a draft, there was no need for any sugar coating.

In the absence of an obviously impending draft, there was no overwhelming sentiment even to give national service much study. Sen. Paul E. Tsongas, D-Mass., a former Peace Corps volunteer, in 1979 introduced a bill to create a presidential commission on national service. Rep. Leon E. Panetta, D-Calif., introduced a similar bill in the House. Tsongas' proposal, in the form of a rider to an unrelated bill, was narrowly approved by the Senate in 1980, but later dropped in a Senate-House conference. Panetta's bill never reached the floor of the House.

However, Rep. Patricia Schroeder, D-Colo., along with McCloskey and Panetta, in 1979 introduced an amendment to the Defense Authorization Act of 1980 that obliged President Carter to conduct a limited study of national service. The president was to look into "the desirability, in the interest of preserving discipline and morale in the Armed Forces, of establishing a national youth service program permitting volunteer work, for either public or private public-service agencies, as an alternative to military service."

In his report in February 1980, Carter found the McCloskey and Cavanaugh national service plans promising, but saw no need for any form of national service at that time. The report contained what national service advocates Eberly and Sherraden have described as "an ominous warning": "Any program that would compete for the same pool of qualified individuals as the military," said Carter's report, "must be viewed as deleterious in its impact on the morale and discipline as well as on the force levels of the Armed Forces as currently staffed." [21]

Danzig and Szanton, in their study, reached a similar conclusion: "Military conscription could work with a civilian alter-

[21] Quoted by Eberly and Sherraden in "Alternative Models of National Service," *op. cit.*, p. 93.

native," they wrote, "but it would not work as well as it would without that alternative. The civilian component would introduce challenges and expenses that otherwise could be avoided." If the all-volunteer force seemed to be failing, conscription with a civilian option might seem better than no conscription at all. "But the Pentagon," the authors said, "probably would prefer conscription without national service." [22]

Despite the doubts and concerns of the late '70s, there was no return to conscription, with or without national service. The nation stayed with the all-volunteer force, and around the turn of the decade, its condition began to improve. Growing unemployment in the civilian economy as the recession deepened was one reason. But there were others: Military pay was raised in 1980 and 1981; educational benefits for recruits were improved; more money was devoted to recruiting, and the military's public image seemed more favorable. "The services recruited record proportions of high school graduates," Binkin wrote, "and retention problems seemed to all but disappear." [23]

In the ensuing years, the economy recovered, the decline in the number of qualified and available 18-year-old males continued, and there were no more large military pay raises. But the military services, Binkin said, still continued to recruit "a record quality." The services "have learned how to recruit," he said, and their success in recent years "augurs well for [the all-volunteer force] surviving the rest of the demographic decline."

In the near future, a return to military conscription is unlikely, in Binkin's view, "unless we see some serious deterioration in U.S.-Soviet relations or, indeed, some kind of a war." There will be no system of national service without conscription, he thinks, and quite possibly none with it, if the government had sufficient popular support in the war or other emergency that prompted the draft's return.

Whether as "sugar coating" for military conscription or as the Jamesian "moral equivalent of war," national service seems likely to remain what it has always been: an attractive abstraction unlikely to be turned into a full-fledged reality. Still, there may be some limited attempts to bring it into being. Mager of Friends of VISTA foresees in the coming years "lots of little local models . . . local service programs, whether they're citywide programs or university-based programs or whatever." And Danzig noted: "I suppose that if I have to bet about national service, I would bet that it'll come in fits and starts, if it comes at all, and that there will be some experimentation."

[22] Danzig and Szanton, *op. cit.*, p. 147. In 1985, Defense Secretary Caspar W. Weinberger and Gen. John W. Vessey Jr., then chairman of the Joint Chiefs of Staff, told a House Foreign Affairs Committee hearing that national service was not needed. Vessey said that "universal service may have a value to the country, but its value is not to the Department of Defense." See *The Washington Post*, Feb. 22, 1985.
[23] Binkin, *op. cit.*, p. 28.

Recommended Reading List

Books

Binkin, Martin, *America's Volunteer Military: Progress and Prospects,* Brookings Institution, 1984.

Danzig, Richard, and Peter Szanton, *National Service: What Would It Mean?,* Lexington Books, 1986.

James, William, "The Moral Equivalent of War," in Bruce W. Wilshire, ed., *William James: The Essential Writings,* State University of New York Press, 1984.

Janowitz, Morris, *The Reconstruction of Patriotism: Education for Civic Consciousness,* University of Chicago Press, 1984.

Rice, Gerard T., *The Bold Experiment: JFK's Peace Corps,* University of Notre Dame Press, 1985.

Sherraden, Michael W., and Donald J. Eberly, eds., *National Service: Social, Economic and Military Impacts,* Pergamon Press, 1982.

Wofford, Harris, *Of Kennedys and Kings: Making Sense of the Sixties,* Farrar Straus Giroux, 1980.

Articles

Butterfield, Fox, "Universities Take Lead in New Volunteer Efforts," *The New York Times,* Oct. 17, 1985.

Cohen, Eliot A., "Why We Need a Draft," *Commentary,* April 1982.

Moskos, Charles C., "Making the All-Volunteer Force Work: A National Service Approach," *Foreign Affairs,* fall 1981.

Peters, Charles, "A Neoliberal's Manifesto," *The Washington Monthly,* May 1983.

Wofford, Harris, "The New Work Begins at Home," *The Nation,* Nov. 30, 1985.

Reports and Studies

Coalition for a Democratic Majority Task Force on Foreign Policy and Defense, "Military Manpower: National Service and the Common Defense," October 1986.

U.S. House of Representatives Subcommittee on Manpower and Housing of the Committee on Government Operations, "ACTION's Rationale for the Proposed Elimination of the VISTA Program," March 23 and 24, 1982.

U.S. House of Representatives Subcommittee on Select Education of the Committee on Education and Labor, "Oversight Hearing on the VISTA Program," June 18, 1985.

Graphics: P. 65 photos, VISTA and U.S. Army; photos p. 67, Jacques Lowe and Peace Corps; photos p. 71, Ken Heinen and Sue Klemens; photo p. 72, Peace Corps; photo p. 75, VISTA; photo p. 79, Wide World; photo p. 81, U.S. Army.

NEW DEAL
FOR
THE FAMILY

by

Robert K. Landers

July 25
1 9 8 6

Editor's Note: Since this report was published, the Reagan administration's Working Group on the Family *(see p. 103)* issued its study. The study, released in November 1896, said that "Although many family problems are not amenable to policy solutions," public officials could attempt to affect contemporary culture by showing intolerance for drug abuse, pornography and anti-religious bigotry. The study warned against misapplying the "pro-family" label to such expensive devices as state-funded day care and national health systems.

The Supreme Court, by a 6-3 vote on Jan. 13, 1987, upheld the California law that required employers to give women maternity leave of up to four months. *(See p. 95).*

NEW DEAL
FOR THE FAMILY

Juggling Motherhood and Jobs

Since the early 1970s, the abstraction that is "the family" has been beset by angry extremists. First, radical feminists reviled it as an instrument of male oppression. Then, in reaction, radicals on the political right carried it into battle in crusades against abortion and other real or perceived evils. So great was the ideological tumult that many people wondered if the venerable institution of the family were not doomed to imminent extinction, a fear that enhanced the strength of "pro-family" activists.

Yet all the while, the actual American family — all the multitudes of particular families existing and coming into existence — was doing what it has always done under the pressure of social and economic change: evolving, adapting, surviving. The result is that today's family seldom resembles the "traditional" abstraction of yesteryear, that family in which father works and mother stays at home with the children. Of the 63.2 million families in America in 1985, less than 10 percent fit that description.[1]

Increasingly, American mothers have been leaving home and children and going to work. Twenty million mothers of children under 18 years old are now in the labor force. Half of the married mothers with children under three are now working outside the home; in 1970 that proportion was only one-fourth.

---

[1] U.S. Labor Department's Bureau of Labor Statistics.

The change has been great and rapid.[2] So rapid, said Rep. Patricia Schroeder, D-Colo., that "it's been hard for politicians and the country to keep up with it." She added: "I find the people are way ahead of the politicians on this. Even my generation, when we grew up, I would say most of the middle-class [mothers] had the option to stay home a couple of years with their children. . . . [T]oday, when you see that just the cost of housing has doubled from '74 to '84, and people's wages didn't, it brings home that very few people have that option anymore. So to have the government continually saying, 'We're pro-family and that means that women should stay in the home and do all these things' — that may be lovely but no one can do it."[3]

The new infusion of mothers of young children into the work force is having far-reaching effects. It is prompting the women's movement to reconsider its quest for equal rights. The argument is increasingly heard that women who are both workers and mothers need society's special help if they are to fulfill both roles. A California case involving maternity leave is pending before the U.S. Supreme Court and has feminists on both sides of the issue (see p. 95). Beyond the feminist argumentation is the reality of social change. The perceived need of working mothers for support — in such forms as day care, parental leave, and "flextime" arrangements which enable parents to have flexible work hours — is beginning to bring about a reshaping of the American work place. And more is at stake than making life easier, or even fairer, for working mothers.

"In the case of women and families," said Rep. Nancy L. Johnson, R-Conn., "there is now developing a sense that if we don't begin to take into account the needs of families, of healthy families, in the making of public policy, then we won't have the kind of society that we value." The increased number of working mothers, she said, "raises two issues: Who's going to take care of the children? And what's the impact on children of nonparental care? And I think we're only just now beginning to become conscious of the fact that our society is going to have to make some changes in response to this changed relationship between employment and family."

The extent to which government will play a role in making those changes is not yet clear. But it is clear that the new working mothers and their needs are giving the Democratic Party an opportunity to get off the defensive about "family

---

[2] See Howard Hayghe, "Rise in Mothers' Labor Force Activity Includes Those with Infants," *Monthly Labor Review,* February 1986. Hayghe is an economist in the U.S. Labor Department's Bureau of Labor Statistics.

[3] Persons quoted in this report were interviewed by the author unless otherwise indicated.

values" and make a broad-based appeal to American families. In the House of Representatives, where the Democrats enjoy a majority, a parental leave measure was approved by two committees in June and is headed for a floor vote. The Republicans, meanwhile, can point to the tax reform measure taking shape in a joint Senate-House conference committee as including the essence of what President Reagan described in May 1985 as "the strongest pro-family initiative in postwar history" *(see p. 99).*

Mothers, Single and Married, Going Off to Work

The statistics are striking. In 1975, about 55 percent of America's children had mothers who did not work outside the home. A decade later, the percentages had reversed, so that 57.5 percent had mothers in the labor force.

Some of the working mothers are single. More than two-thirds of the approximately six million single-parent mothers with children under 18 were working outside the home in 1985. Nearly 45 percent of the single mothers with children under 3 were out working. Between 1975 and 1985, the number of children in single-parent families swelled by almost 27 percent, to 12.6 million, and more than half had mothers who worked in 1985. Francine D. Blau, an economist at the University of Illinois, said the increased number of single mothers is mainly due to the rising divorce rate, although the increased number of

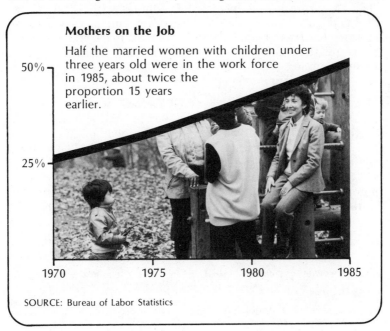

Mothers on the Job

Half the married women with children under three years old were in the work force in 1985, about twice the proportion 15 years earlier.

50%

25%

1970   1975   1980   1985

SOURCE: Bureau of Labor Statistics

births to unmarried women is also a factor contributing to the trend.[4]

Most of the working mothers, however, are married. In 1985, more than three-fifths of the 24.2 million married women with children under 18 were in the labor force. That proportion 15 years earlier was less than two-fifths. But the greatest proportional increase in married mothers who work came among those with young children. Half with children under three were working in 1985, and nearly half with children one or under were working; 15 years earlier, the proportion in both cases was about one-fourth. By 1985, there were more than 26 million children in married-couple families whose mothers worked outside the home.

Economic Necessity Is Major Motivating Force

In all, nearly 33.5 million children in 1985 had mothers who worked. Many of these children doubtless asked a pertinent question: Why? The answer seems largely to be: perceived economic necessity. A 1983 *New York Times* poll showed that for 71 percent of mothers who worked, their reason for doing so was not "for something interesting to do," not "to earn extra money," but rather to "support their family."[5] That support was much needed, according to a 1985 study done for Congress' Joint Economic Committee.

The study, by Sheldon Danziger and Peter Gottschalk,[6] found that the average real income for families with children has declined since 1973, while the poverty rate among families with children has risen. Female-headed families, in general, are much worse off than married-couple families, but even for the two-parent families, the working mothers' income has become extremely important.

For all families with children, the average income in constant (1984) dollars rose from $28,369 in 1967 to $32,206 in 1973, then declined to $29,527 in 1984. For female-headed families, average real income fell 7.8 percent, to $13,257, between 1973 and 1984, while income for two-parent families dropped by 3.1 percent, to $34,379. The gap between female-headed families and two-parent families was much wider than the one between black and white families. "In 1984 black two-parent families had about 80 percent of the income of white two-parent families," Danziger and Gottschalk noted. "But the mean income for white female-

---

[4] Testimony given to the House Select Committee on Children, Youth and Families, April 17, 1986.

[5] Cited in "Working Mothers are Preserving Family Living Standards," a staff study for Congress' Joint Economic Committee, May 9, 1986, p. 2.

[6] Sheldon Danziger and Peter Gottschalk, "How Have Families with Children Been Faring?," November 1985. Danziger is a professor of social work and director of the Institute for Research on Poverty at the University of Wisconsin-Madison. Gottschalk is an associate professor of economics at Bowdoin College.

headed families was only about 40 percent of that of white two-parent families and a little more than half of that of black two-parent families." [7]

However, looking at the average income of families with children obscures the fact that low- and middle-income families' share of the economic pie shrank between 1967 and 1984, while upper-income families' share increased. "Poverty for all persons living in families with children," Danziger and Gottschalk said, "declined between 1967 and 1973, increased somewhat between 1973 and 1979, and then increased rapidly between 1979 and 1984. Black two-parent families were the only group to deviate much from this trend — their 1984 poverty rate, 19.3 percent, was substantially below their 1967 rate, 31.3 percent." The greatest differences in poverty rates, as in family incomes, were between two-parent and female-headed families. And the number of female-headed families was increasing among all races.

In 1965, in his then-controversial report, "The Negro Family: The Case for National Action," Daniel Patrick Moynihan asserted that the United States was "approaching a new crisis in race relations," because 21 percent of non-white families in 1960 were families with a female head.[8] Sen. Moynihan, D-N.Y., commented last year in lectures at Harvard that have recently been published: "By 1984 the census would report that for white families with children this proportion had reached nearly 20

---

[7] Black two-parent families, in fact, have made great gains since 1967, their average income increasing by 28 percent between 1967 and 1973, and by 3.9 percent between 1973 and 1984, according to Danziger and Gottschalk.

[8] The 1965 Moynihan report is included in Lee Rainwater and William L. Yancey, *The Moynihan Report and the Politics of Controversy* (1967).

CATHY CATHY GUISEWITE

Copyright, 1986, Universal Press Syndicate. Reprinted with permission. All rights reserved.

percent. . . . [W]hat was a crisis condition for the one group in 1960 is now the general condition." [9]

Plight of Married Mothers Turned Single Parents

Many single mothers are living with their children in conditions worse than they had previously known, and with little hope of improvement. Nearly 65 percent of the female heads of families in 1984 had been divorced or separated, and more than 10 percent were widows. "Thus, the vast majority of children currently living in families headed by their mothers previously lived in two-parent families which had, on average, much higher average incomes," according to Danziger and Gottschalk. The persistent pay gap between men and women, whatever its causes, suddenly becomes overwhelmingly relevant to many married mothers who become single parents. [10]

Stanford sociologist Lenore J. Weitzman studied the effects of California's widely hailed no-fault divorce law, and found that the effect of the average divorce decree was to decrease the standard of living of the woman and any minor children in her household by 73 percent, while increasing the man's standard of living by 42 percent. [11] Behind all the statistics about the hard-pressed single mothers are, of course, real people, such as one New Hampshire woman who, after 23 years of marriage and eight children, was left by her husband for a younger woman; her family's income plummeted from $70,000 a year to just over $7,000. [12]

Most women at the head of families were working, and their average earnings were increasing. Yet the average real income of these women declined by 6.5 percent between 1967 and 1984. Among the reasons, according to Danziger and Gottschalk, were decreased earnings by other household members and decreased welfare benefits, which are not indexed to inflation.

During those same years, the average real income of two-parent families with children increased by 14.1 percent. According to Danziger and Gottschalk, the "major factor" behind that increase was the increased earnings of wives. "If wives' earnings had not increased between 1967 and 1984," they concluded, "mean family income would have grown more slowly and pov-

[9] Daniel Patrick Moynihan, *Family and Nation* (1986), p. 146. The proportion of female-headed families is still far greater for blacks, however: In 1984, two parents were present in less than 45 percent of all black families with children, according to Danziger and Gottschalk.

[10] The median income of year-round, full-time male workers in 1984 was $24,004; the comparable figure for women was $15,422. See "Women's Economic Equity," *E.R.R.*, 1985 Vol. I, pp. 333-356.

[11] Cited by Marianne Takas, "Divorce: Who Gets the Blame in 'No Fault'?" *Ms.*, February 1986, pp. 48-50.

[12] The woman's story is recounted by Ruth Sidel in *Women and Children Last: The Plight of Poor Women in Affluent America* (1986), pp. 27-28.

erty and income inequality would have increased more rapidly
than they actually did."

Feminists Reconsider Aims

In her landmark 1963 book, *The Feminine Mystique,* Betty
Friedan grimly likened the situation of a suburban American
housewife in her home to that of a prisoner in a Nazi concentration camp. Twenty years later, Friedan was reveling in her new
role of grandmother, marveling at the strength of women's
desire to bear children, and reflecting on "the revolution that
book helped spark." Thanks to the women's movement, she said
in a magazine article, "the feminine mystique, which defined
women only as husband's wife, children's mother, server of the
family's physical needs and never as person," had been "tran-
scended." But now, she said, women had "come about as far as
we could with the male model of equity" and needed "a model
encompassing female experience and female values, which men
are beginning to share." Women now needed to move their
revolution to a "second stage," and to "come to terms with
family and with work." [13]

"Now that economic necessity dictates that most women
must continue to work after they become mothers...," she
wrote, "someone is going to have to battle in a new and serious
way, for institutions that will help the new family." She called

[13] Betty Friedan, "Twenty Years After *The Feminine Mystique,*" *The New York Times
Magazine,* Feb. 27, 1983, p. 35. In her 1981 book, *The Second Stage,* Friedan noted (p. 28)
that she had "resorted to a rather extreme metaphor" when she said that the housewife was
in a "comfortable concentration camp" in 1963.

for "imaginative thinking" about such matters as maternity leave, time off for parents when their children are sick, flextime and "child-care supports that don't now exist."

Friedan had been founder of the National Organization for Women (NOW) and its first president; her feminist credentials were impeccable. But that did not mean that the women's movement would accept her new analysis or rush to embrace the family. Dana Friedman, now a senior research associate with The Conference Board, a non-profit business research organization, for years lobbied for a better system of child care for working mothers. She said she could never get NOW or several other women's groups to "actively promote or lend their resources to the issue. It was so frustrating."

The women's movement, she said, in its push for equal rights, had made a far greater effort "to help women who don't want to have children, i.e., gay women and those who want abortions, than [to help] those who do [want to have children]." Friedman said that the women's movement had striven to avoid "anything that smacks of motherhood and kids. . . . And that was, in my estimation, probably a tactical error. Maybe necessary at the time, but, in retrospect, I think it's what created [anti-feminist leader] Phyllis Schlafly's constituency,[14] because she tapped a nerve for all the women who were at home, who chose to be at home with their kids, [the women] that the women's movement didn't embrace."

Economist Sylvia Ann Hewlett, a feminist as well as a wife and mother, declares in her 1986 book, *A Lesser Life*, that the women's movement in the United States "has not just been anti-men; it has also been profoundly anti-children and anti-motherhood." American feminists have concentrated on obtaining equal rights with men. In contrast, Hewlett says, feminists in Western Europe have seen woman's main problem as "her dual burden — in the home and in the work force." European feminists, therefore, have sought to lighten "this load by instituting family support systems." European feminism, she says, has had at its core "a practical concern with the concrete conditions of women's lives. This social feminist tradition is almost totally absent in modern America." [15]

Hewlett contends that the women's movement here has failed to face the fact that women are not men, that only women can have babies. "To ignore this biological difference, as many American feminists do," she writes, "is to commit a double folly.

---

[14] Schlafly rallied opposition in the nation to the Equal Rights Amendment and other feminist causes. She first came to public notice during the 1964 Republican presidential campaign of Sen. Barry Goldwater, with a tract called *A Choice Not an Echo.*
[15] Sylvia Ann Hewlett, *A Lesser Life: The Myth of Women's Liberation in America* (1986), pp. 185, 217, 174.

In the first place, it ensures that most women will become second-class citizens in the workplace. For *without public support policies few women can cope with motherhood without hopelessly compromising their career goals* [author's emphasis]. Secondly, society has to suffer. For a child cannot be compared with a new car or a vacation, some private consumer good that a woman can choose to spend resources on if the fancy strikes her. The decision to have a child is both a private and a public decision, for children are our collective future. If we fail to create decent conditions for the bearing of children, and if we deprive these children of parental contact in the first few weeks of life, we will pay a huge price in the future."

Lawsuit Over Maternity Leave Divides Feminists

The idea that women require special treatment from society is now dividing American feminists. The split is evident, for example, in a California case involving maternity leave that is pending before the U.S. Supreme Court. In 1982, Lillian Garland, a receptionist at the California Federal Savings and Loan Association in Los Angeles, tried to go back to work two months after giving birth to a child, and was told that her job was filled. Garland complained to the state's Fair Employment and Housing Department, accusing California Federal of violating a state law requiring employers to give women maternity leaves of up to four months. The savings and loan association (which did eventually give Garland a job similar to the one she had), along with the state Chamber of Commerce and the Merchants and Manufacturers Association, went to federal court to challenge the state law, contending that it illegally discriminated against men. The court agreed and overturned the maternity-leave law. But an appellate court reversed that ruling.

CATHY CATHY GUISEWITE

Copyright, 1986, Universal Press Syndicate. Reprinted with permission. All rights reserved.

NOW and the American Civil Liberties Union (ACLU) are opposed to the California law, while Betty Friedan and other feminists have rallied behind the statute. "We don't think women are weak and in need of special assistance in that way," Joan Bertin, associate director of the ACLU's Women's Rights Project, said of the California law. "Obviously the work place must accommodate pregnancy and the needs of parents," she said, "but I believe the central issue is that people shouldn't be fired for absence from work because of any temporary disability, whether it's pregnancy or a hernia." She has asked the Supreme Court to interpret the California law so as to provide up to four months' unpaid leave for any disabled worker.

Friedan, on the other hand, said, "The time has come to acknowledge that women are different from men, and that there has to be a concept of equality that takes into account that women are the ones who have the babies. We shouldn't be stuck with always using a male model, trying to twist pregnancy into something that's like a hernia. At a minimum, women should not be fired because they get pregnant. That's minimal." [16] The Supreme Court is expected to hear arguments in the California case in the fall.

Beyond the feminist debate is the reality that working women face. Many large companies do provide maternity or parental leave. A survey of 384 large companies by Catalyst, a New York non-profit research organization, found that about half offered women unpaid leaves after disability leaves. But policies vary widely, and most women work for companies that do not provide even disability leaves. [17] There is no national policy on maternity or parental leave. A bill sponsored by Rep. William L. Clay, D-Mo., Rep. Schroeder and others — the 1986 Family and Medical Leave Act — would require employers with 15 or more workers to provide both mothers and fathers up to 18 weeks of unpaid leave to care for newborn or newly adopted children, or seriously ill children or parents. The measure is opposed by the Chamber of Commerce of the United States and other business groups, but it was approved by two House committees in June.

Schroeder argues that parental leave involves more than the mother's physical health. "It's the child's emotional stability in those first three to four months — [that's] absolutely critical in the 'bonding' process with either parent. . . . We know all these things, and yet we've got people out there working who have to

---

[16] Bertin and Friedan are quoted by Tamar Lewin in *The New York Times,* June 28, 1986.

[17] The 1978 Pregnancy Discrimination Act requires companies with 15 or more employees to provide the same disability benefits for a pregnancy-related absence as they would for any other medical leave. Companies that provide no disability payments, however, need not provide any when childbirth is involved.

work and if they're told to return to work in two weeks, six weeks, or whatever, what do they do? The crisis they go through is phenomenal."

Parental leave, Rep. Johnson said, is "definitely coming, and it's one of those things like having access to appropriate day care that is essential if we're going to have healthy families." She said that when "the consequences of not allowing families to get on their feet . . . of not allowing parents to be home when a child is sick," are weighed against "the inconvenience and cost of a more flexible parental leave policy for eight or 10 years in an employee's life, out of a productive work life of 40 years, it doesn't make sense not to readjust our personnel policies and our employment structure to account for the needs of families."

The Chamber of Commerce has argued that mandatory parental leave policy would be "contrary to the voluntary, flexible and comprehensive benefit system that the private sector has developed." [18] Schroeder said, "I don't see it as a 'benefit.' I see it as a labor standard, just like health and safety, occupational safety, wage-and-hour. . . . We're talking about leave without pay, absolutely bare minimum. . . ."

U.S. Lagging in Parental Leave, Day-Care Policies

In contrast to the United States, most industrialized nations have national maternity or parental leave policies. They also, according to Hewlett, have made "considerable progress" with respect to public or publicly-funded child care. In the United States, however, there is no national day-care policy. And, according to a report by the House Select Committee on Children, Youth and Families, chaired by Rep. George Miller, D-Calif., "there are very large gaps in current [child-care] services.

---

[18] Quoted by Julie Rovner in "House Committee Approves Guaranteed Family Leave Bill," *Congressional Quarterly Weekly Report*, June 28, 1986, p. 1485.

Waiting lists for family day care homes and centers for infants and after-school programs for school-aged children are commonplace. . . . Even preschool care, the most widely available of all child care, is inadequate in many communities." [19]

The committee report discerned "much potential in private sector assistance," but said it is still "an almost completely untapped resource." Friedman of The Conference Board estimates that about 3,000 U.S. employers, most of them larger ones, currently provide some form of child-care support to their workers. She said that about 150 companies, 400 hospitals and 50 public agencies offer on-site day-care centers; about 300 companies arrange discounts for their employees who use specific care-providers; about 500 companies provide information and referral services, and about 1,500 offer so-called flexible benefits, which include non-taxable child-care assistance as an option.

Friedman said she has found that employers generally seem "more willing to help their employees buy into the existing system of child care by helping them find it or pay for it, than they are [interested] in creating the services." That increases the importance of the system of child care available outside the companies, she noted. "And that's why I think government still has an enormous role to play, not only in meeting the needs of parents but in helping and encouraging companies to get involved. The notion that the less the government does, the more companies will do, just doesn't work."

Government in certain respects has been doing less, at least for low- and moderate-income families. Before 1981, Title 20 of the Social Security Act provided funds to states specifically to help such families pay for child care. "When Title 20 was incorporated into the Social Services Block Grant as a result of the 1981 Omnibus Budget Reconciliation Act," the Select Committee recounts, "funding levels were reduced by 21 percent, and the targeted $200 million in federal funds for child care were eliminated.

"Supporting services, like the child care nutrition program, have also been reduced. As a result, the majority of states have reduced their child care services for low and moderate income families." However, the federal child-care tax credit [20] has been

---

[19] Select Committee on Children, Youth and Families, "Families and Child Care: Improving the Options," September 1984, p. *ix*. See "Day-Care Needs," *E.R.R.*, 1983 Vol. I, pp. 333-352.

[20] The federal tax code provides a credit to working parents who incur child-care expenses. Before the law was changed in 1982, it provided a credit of 20 percent of expenses incurred, up to a maximum of $2,000 for one dependent and $4,000 for two or more. In 1982, the credit was increased to 30 percent for taxpayers with incomes of $10,000 or less, with the credit reduced by 1 percentage point for each $2,000 of income between $10,000 and $28,000. The limits on eligible expenses were increased to $2,400 for one dependent and $4,800 for two or more.

increasingly used, providing an estimated $1.7 billion in 1984 to families who had child-care expenses. Still, according to the Select Committee, two-thirds of the tax credit relief goes to families with above-median incomes, and "none goes to the millions of families who lack sufficient disposable income to take advantage" of the credit.

Whatever government's role should be regarding day care or parental leave, the number of American women now struggling with the dual burden of job and family is too large to be ignored. Change clearly is coming, not only to the women's movement, but to the American work place. Rep. Johnson, a moderate Republican, said she thinks that "outside of the day-care subsidy issue, the most important issues are going to be dealt with out there in the private sector. And I think they're going to be dealt with, because companies are going to have to compete for women employees and for male employees who take their family responsibilities seriously and who have greater family responsibilities because their wife is working. So I do think that this whole issue of family leave policies and flexible work hours and all of these things are going to become operative as companies compete for employees. I begin to see that happening already."

Social analyst and author Ben J. Wattenberg agrees: "I think an awful lot of this is going to happen organically, when you move into the 1990s and you end up with labor shortages,[21] that companies are going to be saying, 'Hey, we'd better have flextime if we want to get the best people, because that's something that certain people really want.'"

Pro-Family Politics

"I believe the worth of any economic policy must be measured by the strength of its commitment to American families, the bedrock of our society." So spoke President Reagan in a speech to the nation on May 28, 1985. He continued: "There is no instrument of hard work, savings and job creation as effective as the family. There is no cultural institution as ennobling as family life. And there is no superior, indeed, no equal means to rear the young, protect the weak or attend the elderly. None.

---

[21] The labor shortages are expected because of the declining number of births during the late 1960s and early 1970s.

"Yet past government policies betrayed families and family values. They permitted inflation to push families relentlessly into higher and higher tax brackets. And not only did the personal exemption fail to keep pace with inflation, in real dollars its actual value dropped dramatically over the last 30 years."

Reagan was proposing a wide-ranging revision of the federal tax code, including what he termed "the strongest pro-family initiative in postwar history," i.e., not only lower tax rates, but a virtual doubling of the income tax exemption for each family member to $2,000, to be indexed against inflation.[22]

In 1948, the personal and dependent exemption was $600. If that exemption had been indexed to the growth in personal income since 1948, it would have risen to about $5,600 in 1984. If the $600 exemption had been indexed to inflation as measured by the Consumer Price Index, it would have risen to $2,589 in 1984. Instead, the personal and dependent exemption grew only to $1,080. In 1948, Sen. Moynihan notes, three-fourths of median family income for a family of four was, in effect, exempt from federal income tax. "Was this not in effect a powerful national family policy? It costs money to raise a fam-

---

[22] The tax reform plans approved by the Senate in June and by the House of Representatives last December essentially retain the $2,000 personal and dependent exemption, although the House version would reduce it to $1,500 for taxpayers who itemize their deductions. A joint Senate-House conference committee this month began writing the final version of the bill.

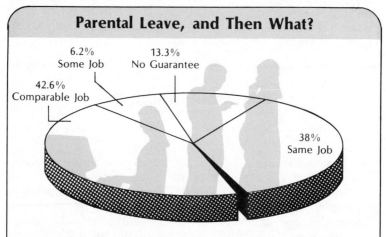

Parental Leave, and Then What?

6.2%
Some Job

13.3%
No Guarantee

42.6%
Comparable Job

38%
Same Job

Most of the large corporations in a parental leave survey by the New York research firm of Catalyst offered women employees some type of job guarantee when they went back to work. But only about two-fifths of the firms offered women their same job.

SOURCE: *Catalyst*

ily, and the federal government chose not to tax most of the income so required. This is no longer so." [23]

If it is less than it could be, Reagan's proposed doubling of the personal and dependent exemption still seems to be a fairly strong "pro-family initiative," evidence at least that Republican enthusiasm for the family is not entirely rhetorical. But in their efforts to compete with Democrats in dealing with the needs of working mothers and their families, conservative Republicans are likely to be hindered by their desire to encourage the "traditional" family (in which the mother does not work outside the home), as well as by their attachments to business and the idea of a free market. And to the "pro-family" activists on the New Right and the Religious Right, economics is far less significant than their agenda of social issues, including opposition to abortion, feminism and homosexual rights, as well as to the absence of official prayer in the schools.

In recent years, conservative Republicans and "pro-family" activists have put the Democrats on the defensive on issues relating to the family. But that may be changing. Rep. Schroeder, recalling that earlier period, said, "When I first came to Congress, I introduced a comprehensive day-care bill along with then-Sen. [Walter F.] Mondale and other members, and we were almost run out of town. It was like it was communism, we were trying to put everybody's kids into day care, and force the mothers to go to work. Why, you couldn't pull that rhetoric off today. The world's changed too much. And that was the early '70s!"

Liberal Democrats Given Political Opportunity

Despite conservatives' enthusiasm for the "traditional" family, American mothers in increasing numbers are working outside the home, largely from perceived economic necessity. Their dual burden is a heavy one, and society has an obvious interest in helping families raise their children well. All this seems to present the Democrats with an opportunity to draw upon their liberal tradition and rush to the rescue of the modern family, middle class as well as poor.

"Throughout modern history," historian Laura Gellott has written, "conservative politicians have appealed to 'family' to fill the void created by the collapse of the familiar guideposts of political order, economic stability, and traditional values. Such appeals are in reality nothing more than the manipulation of fears of an uncertain future, and the fear of social change which often manifests itself in the form of emancipation for women. . . . Liberals need to appropriate the idea of family as a

---

[23] See Moynihan, *Family and Nation*, pp. 158-160.

source of identity by putting it at the service, not of nostalgia for the past, but anticipation of the future. It is the sense of family as a commitment to the future that is essential here." [24]

"The perception," Schroeder said, "was ... the Republicans stole the [family] issue and the Democrats had nothing to say on it. The Republicans, you notice, for all their talk about the [family] issue ... then end up voting against all these [family-related] issues, as many of them have been; then it's like one talks and the other produces. I think people [will] go with the producers." Whether that is so or not, the new infusion of mothers into the labor force is at least giving Democrats a chance to get off the "pro-family" defensive and to compete with Republicans for the favor of families dwelling in the political center.

The Republicans, of course, are not willing to yield the family, even the poor family, to their opponents. The president, in his State of the Union address last February, announced that the White House Domestic Council would be conducting "an evaluation of programs and a strategy for immediate action to meet the financial, educational, social, and safety concerns of poor families." Not long after, a working group on the family was appointed, with Education Under Secretary Gary L. Bauer at its head. The task force is to submit its report to the White House Domestic Council by Nov. 1 (which, by coincidence or not, is three days before Election Day).

"Not surprisingly," Bauer said, "we are finding a prejudice that we brought to this being confirmed, and that is that a good bit of what one can identify as being bad for the family over the last 25 years has cultural roots to it. That's not to say that government hasn't made it worse by the messages government has sent through one policy or another. But there are many things that need to be addressed that will not lend themselves directly to government action."

Although "some extremely traditional conservatives" would argue against government providing a tax credit for day care, on the ground that it "entices women to leave the home," Bauer said, he himself sees "nothing wrong with that credit, but it shouldn't discriminate the way it does now. ... I mean why not a credit to help families take care of children ... whether the mother works outside the home or whether the mother decides to take care of the children in the home herself? ... That's not to say that under the current fiscal situation we could expand the credit that way, but it's an idea of where I come from on some of these things."

---

[24] Laura Gellott, "Staking Claim to the Family," *Commonweal*, Sept. 20, 1985, p. 491.

Conservatives Focus on the 'Traditional' Family

Government's assistance to working mothers is likely to be extremely limited indeed, if it must always be balanced by an equal amount of assistance given to mothers not working outside the home. "There is concern among the conservatives," noted Rep. Johnson, "that somehow if you provide services, you encourage the woman to leave the home, and thereby encourage

People "feel very strongly that it's about time Congress woke up" on family issues, says Rep. Patricia Schroeder, D-Colo.

the erosion of the family. I simply don't buy that. A day-care subsidy is never going to cover the full cost of day care. And you're not going to make the choice to go to work because day care is available and the day-care subsidy can help you."

Beyond the ideological battles that have raged over the family in recent years, the sheer demographic facts now seem to guarantee that increasing attention will be paid to the needs of working mothers and their children. Schroeder said she thinks that family policy issues are "going to become much more important because the people are really struggling with it, and I think these are not issues that there are big political action committees behind, but they [people] feel very strongly that it's about time Congress woke up and caught up . . . with the whole rest of the world."

Johnson said she thinks what happens depends on how readily business adapts. "It depends on how rapidly they see it in their interest, and how successful they are in finding policies that address it. If they do a very good job, then I think the change will take place without a lot of public discussion. If they resist and try to stay within the old 9-to-5 mold and pregnancy is non-existent as far as we're concerned and so are children and families and anything outside the work place, then there will be much more struggle and much more legislating."

Recommended Reading List

Books

Caplow, Theodore *et al.*, *Middletown Families: Fifty Years of Change and Continuity*, University of Minnesota, 1982.
Friedan, Betty, *The Second Stage*, Summit, 1981.
Hewlett, Sylvia Ann, *A Lesser Life: The Myth of Women's Liberation in America*, Morrow, 1986.
Moynihan, Daniel Patrick, *Family and Nation*, Harcourt Brace Jovanovich, 1986.
——, "The Case for a Family Policy," in *Coping: Essays on the Practice of Government*, Random House, 1973.
Sidel, Ruth, *Women and Children Last: The Plight of Poor Women in Affluent America*, Viking, 1986.
Steiner, Gilbert Y., *The Futility of Family Policy*, Brookings, 1981.

Articles

Brownstein, Ronald, "Everyone's Claiming Family Values: Apple Pie Fight," *The New Republic*, Feb. 3, 1986.
Carlson, Allan C., "What Happened to the 'Family Wage'?," *The Public Interest*, spring 1986.
Friedan, Betty, "Twenty Years After The Feminine Mystique," *The New York Times Magazine*, Feb. 27, 1983.
Gellott, Laura, "Staking Claim to the Family," *Commonweal*, Sept. 20, 1985.
Kantrowitz, Barbara *et al.*, "A Mother's Choice," *Newsweek*, March 31, 1986.
Loury, Glenn C., "The Family, the Nation, and Senator Moynihan," *Commentary*, June 1986.
Rothman, Robert, "Democrats in Congress Open New Push for Child Care Aid," *Congressional Quarterly Weekly Report*, Jan. 11, 1986.
Takas, Marianne, "Divorce: Who Gets the Blame in 'No Fault'?," *Ms.*, February 1986.
Wickenden, Dorothy, "The Women's Movement Looks Beyond 'Equality': What NOW?," *The New Republic*, May 5, 1986.

Reports and Studies

Danziger, Sheldon and Peter Gottschalk, "How Have Families with Children Been Faring?," a study done for the Joint Economic Committee of the Congress, November 1985.
Editorial Research Reports: "Day-Care Needs," 1983 Vol. I, p. 333.
——, "Women's Economic Equity," 1985 Vol. I, p. 333.
U.S. House of Representatives Select Committee on Children, Youth, and Families, "Families and Child Care: Improving the Options," September 1984.
——, "Tax Policy: How Do Families Fare?," October 1985.

Graphics: P. 85 photos, Eastman Kodak Co. and Sue Klemens; cartoons, Cathy Guisewite; chart, p. 89 Bob Redding; chart, p. 100 Kathleen Ossenfort; photo, p. 103, Teresa Zabala.

THE REHNQUIST COURT

Right Turn?

by Elder Witt

**Sept. 26
1 9 8 6**

Editor's Note: The Supreme Court's turn to the right, which was so freely predicted upon William H. Rehnquist's elevation to chief justice and Antonin Scalia's appointment, has not become readily apparent in the 1986-87 term. Scalia's voting pattern was not predictably conservative, and the court's liberal bloc prevailed in several important decisions. The leader of that bloc, Justice William J. Brennan Jr., who reached his 81st birthday on April 25, so far has written majority opinions in five of the important cases this term.

Wooing Conservative Votes

Time was running out when President Reagan finally got his chance to reshape the Supreme Court into the conservative bench he wishes to bequeath to the nation when he leaves the White House.

Despite predictions dating back to Reagan's first year of office that the advanced age of several sitting justices virtually assured him several Supreme Court appointments, it was not until six years into his presidency that Reagan got the opportunity to place his second justice on the bench, thereby giving the court's conservative wing what could be a decisive force in split decisions.

On balance, the administration's effort to advance its conservative social agenda in the Supreme Court that was presided over by Chief Justice Warren E. Burger until his retirement in September has been far from a sterling success. In the past two years, the court has rebuffed the Reagan administration's call for change on several key social issues, including school prayer, affirmative action and abortion.

The role of Sandra Day O'Connor, Reagan's first appointment to the high court, during this period illustrates the riskiness of predicting a justice's voting pattern once the justice is elevated to the high court. Tapped by Reagan in 1981, O'Connor brought to the court's conservative wing an articulate conservative voice that was in harmony with the administration's ideology, but her addition alone was not enough to put the court's conservatives in control. Moreover, in recent years O'Connor has turned in an increasingly independent voting record, siding on occasion with the liberal wing of the court that handed the administration defeats on such high-profile issues as prayer in school and affirmative action.

With Burger's announcement in June that he would retire, Reagan was given a crucial opportunity to further rearrange the court's membership. This opportunity was a dual one because Reagan could both designate a new chief justice, thus securing the special powers of that office in chosen hands, as well as bring a brand new vote onto the court.

For chief justice, Reagan selected William H. Rehnquist, a staunch conservative who was appointed almost 15 years ago by President Nixon. After a noisy but probably foredoomed effort by Senate Democrats to discredit Rehnquist's commitment to civil rights, he was confirmed as expected by the Republican-controlled Senate Sept. 17. As the court's newest justice, Reagan chose Antonin Scalia, a conservative federal appeals court judge with a reputation for an awesome legal intellect and a talent for consensus-building. Scalia's nomination sailed through Senate confirmation Sept. 17.

On the eve of the new court's first term, beginning Oct. 6, the question of how Rehnquist's elevation and Scalia's arrival will affect the court's collective view of the Constitution looms at least as large in the minds of observers as the big lineup of cases on its docket, which includes challenges to Reagan's use of the pocket veto, to state laws requiring "closed" primary elections and to affirmative action plans.

Because of the strong similarity in the views of Rehnquist, Burger and Scalia, a sudden shift in the court's stance on key issues appears unlikely. But personal chemistry among the justices will be a significant factor, especially on a court that in recent years has been closely divided in many of its opinions. In this aspect the makeup of the Rehnquist court may produce a shift in the balance of power toward the conservative wing.

In the Rehnquist court, as in the Burger court, much will depend on the art of persuasion among the justices, as the court's conservative and liberal wings try to woo crucial swing votes on key issues, notably those of Justices Byron R. White, Lewis F. Powell Jr. and O'Connor. In the past, Rehnquist has not been notably successful in winning support for his position, dissenting alone more than any other justice *(See box, pp. 110-111)*. But that could change if he opted to strike a more politic attitude as chief justice.

Scalia, on the other hand, already has the reputation for being an artful persuader, which suggests that he will be an asset to the court's conservative wing from the outset. Both men are considered personable and get along well with their colleagues.

Thus, while conservative domination of the high court is by no means assured, it is, perhaps, within grasp for the first time in half a century. If Rehnquist and Scalia become an effective team, they could build a conservative coalition that could dominate the court, speculates University of Virginia law Professor A. E. Dick Howard, a close observer of the court. At the very least, the pressure of debate is likely to rise on the Rehnquist court. "The tempo of the debate will pick up this term," Howard predicted, "intensifying the pressure on [the] justices in the middle to choose sides."

Rehnquist: Tough Opinions, Easy Manner

In selecting a chief justice to lead his conservative campaign inside the conference room of the Supreme Court, Reagan chose a known quantity in Rehnquist. In almost 15 years on the court, he has voiced his views on hundreds of issues. Most of the time they have coincided with Reagan's own belief in a limited judicial role and a literal approach to the Constitution.

Federal judges, Reagan argues, should not be policy makers. That is the job of elected officials in the executive and legislative branches. Judges should simply tell these lawmakers when they overstep their proper roles. Reagan views the Constitution as the source of government's power — and of limits on those powers. Because he asserts a belief in limited government, he tends to read the Constitution's restrictive provisions literally — and wants judges he appoints to do the same.

In his opinions, Rehnquist, who turns 62 Oct. 1, has consistently argued for a posture of judicial restraint. He argues that the Supreme Court should be the brakes, not the accelerator on the engine of government. The courts are simply there to halt trends that violate the Constitution.

A native of Wisconsin with degrees from Stanford and Harvard universities, Rehnquist became the youngest justice on the court when he was picked by Nixon in 1971. Previously, Rehnquist had served for two-and-a-half years as assistant attorney general in charge of the office of legal counsel under Attorney General John N. Mitchell.

On the court, Rehnquist quickly staked out his position as its most extreme justice. He has, notes John P. Frank, another close observer of the court who writes frequently on the subject, "an amazingly integrated view of the universe to which all issues relate." In one of Rehnquist's first decisions, he criticized the majority's view that there were certain "fundamental personal rights" protected — even if not mentioned — by the Constitution. That position is the basis of his consistent objection to

Rehnquist in Dissent . . .

As the Supreme Court has rebuffed the Reagan administration's conservative policy initiatives, Justice William H. Rehnquist — in dissent — has staunchly defended them.

A look at six of these cases reveals that the core of the court's resistance to the administration's arguments is the quartet of William J. Brennan Jr., Thurgood Marshall, Harry A. Blackmun and John Paul Stevens.

For example, they became a majority on busing by attracting the vote of Byron R. White; on tax exemptions for discriminatory schools by getting everyone's vote but Rehnquist's; on school prayer by winning Lewis F. Powell Jr. and Sandra Day O'Connor; and on abortion, affirmative action, and state aid to parochial schools by winning Powell's vote.

In 1982, the court struck down a Washington state law forbidding local school boards voluntarily to adopt busing as a means of desegregating public schools. The administration had defended the law. In dissent from this decision in *Washington v. Seattle School Dis-*

. . . on the Reagan Side

trict #1, Rehnquist joined an opinion written by Powell, who called this decision an "unprecedented intrusion into the structure of a state government."

The following year, the court affirmed the authority of the Internal Revenue Service (IRS) to deny tax-exempt status to discriminatory private schools. Rehnquist dissented alone, agreeing with the Reagan administration that the IRS lacked this power until Congress amended the law to grant it.

"Congress has the power to further this policy [of opposition to racial discrimination] by denying . . . [tax-exempt] status to organizations that practice racial discrimination," he wrote in *Bob Jones University v. United States.* "But as of yet Congress has failed to do so. Whatever the reasons for that failure, this Court should not legislate for Congress."

In 1985, the court held unconstitutional Alabama's moment-of-silence law, finding that it was intended to provide a state-sanctioned time for prayer in public school classrooms. In dissent in *Wallace v. Jaffree,* Rehnquist argued that the amendment was "designed to prohibit the establishment of a national religion, and perhaps to prevent discrimination among sects . . . [but] not . . . requiring neutrality on the part of government between religion and irreligion."

When the court struck down two different state aid to parochial schools programs in 1985 — in *Aguilar v. Felton,* a New York case, and *Grand Rapids School District v. Ball,* a Michigan case — finding too much symbolic support of parochial education by the state, Rehnquist dissented again. "We have indeed traveled far afield from the concerns which prompted the adoption of the First Amendment when we rely on gossamer abstractions to invalidate a law which obviously meets an entirely secular need," he wrote in the New York case.

This year, the court reaffirmed its view that the Constitution protects a woman's right to an abortion from undue state interference. In so doing, it rejected the administration's suggestion that it leave this issue entirely to the states.

Rehnquist dissented in the Pennsylvania case of *Thornburgh v. American College of Obstetricians and Gynecologists,* joining Justice White's opinion urging the court to overrule the entire line of decisions recognizing this right.

And when the court refused to discard affirmative action as a remedy for racial bias in the workplace, Rehnquist dissented again in the New York/New Jersey case of *Local 28 of the Sheet Metal Workers' International Association v. Equal Employment Opportunity Commission.* The 1964 Civil Rights Act, he argued — as the administration had — "forbids a court from ordering racial preferences that effectively displace non-minorities except to minority individuals who have been the actual victims of a particular employer's racial discrimination."

rulings denying states the power to ban or regulate abortions.[1]

Protesting the court's 1972 decision to strike down existing capital punishment laws on a variety of constitutional grounds, Rehnquist emphasized his belief that over the long run, it is more important for the court to defer to the other branches of the government than to vindicate the rights of particular individuals. It is a mistake for judges to strike down a law in order to protect the rights of an individual, he wrote, because the result "is ... to impose upon the nation the judicial fiat of a majority of a court of judges whose connection with the popular will is remote at best." [2]

In the years that followed, Rehnquist has consistently sounded these themes, often in dissent. He has dissented by himself 47 times — more than any other sitting justice. Eleven of those lone dissents have been in criminal cases, 12 in cases applying the equal protection guarantee to laws challenged as discriminating against aliens, women or illegitimate children, and 10 in First Amendment cases.[3]

Rehnquist alone among his colleagues is completely at ease with the Reagan administration's argument that the original intent of the men who wrote the Constitution and the Bill of Rights is the proper standard for applying that document.

When the court in 1983 struck down a law instituting the observation of a moment of silence in public schools as an abridgment of the First Amendment guarantee of separation of church and state, he dissented.

"It is impossible to build sound constitutional doctrine upon a mistaken understanding of constitutional history," he argued, criticizing as a "misleading metaphor" Thomas Jefferson's often-quoted statement that the First Amendment built "a wall of separation between church and State." [4]

Arguing for the moment of silence and against complete separation, Rehnquist contended that the majority held an erroneous view of the Establishment Clause. That clause, he said, was intended simply to prevent Congress from establishing a national religion, citing as his authority James Madison's remarks on the House floor in 1789, when Congress was considering whether to approve the First Amendment. "Congress should not establish a religion and enforce the legal observation of it by law, nor compel men to worship God in any manner contrary to their conscience," Madison said.

---

[1] *Weber v. Aetna Casualty & Surety Co.* (1972).
[2] *Furman v. Georgia* (1972).
[3] *National Law Journal,* June 30, 1986, pp. 48-49.
[4] *Wallace v. Jaffree,* June 4, 1985, dissenting opinion.

In comparison with Burger, Rehnquist's views on legal issues are similar. The two agreed on at least three out of four cases every term, and in recent terms almost nine of 10 cases.[5]

In style, however, Rehnquist and Burger are very different personalities, and that difference is expected to result in an immediate change in the atmosphere of the court. Burger is a rather formal man, while Rehnquist is informal in his dress, his manner and his general approach. In a characteristic contrast, Burger adamantly opposed televising public sessions of the court, while Rehnquist has said he would be open to the idea. Burger had many difficulties in his relationships on the court. Bruce Fein, an adjunct scholar at the American Enterprise Institute of Public Policy Research (AEI), described Burger as a "porcupine" at a July 1986 AEI seminar. Rehnquist, however, is universally liked by his colleagues.

"The court will surely be a more congenial place," under Rehnquist, comments Howard. "On balance, it will be a friendlier place, more like the days of Earl Warren [chief justice 1953-69], and that may take some edge off the ideological passions" that Rehnquist's promotion is certain to generate.

Rehnquist probably will view the administrative aspects of his new job as less absorbing than did Burger, who devoted a great deal of time and energy to issues of judicial efficiency and reform, arguing frequently that the court was overworked and needed relief.

Although Rehnquist has generally supported the idea that Congress might create a new judicial panel to assist the Supreme Court with some of its work, he does not share the view that it is overworked. His own regular office hours are from 9 a.m. to 3 p.m.

Scalia: Smart, New, Independent Voice

Even before his selection in June, attention began focusing on Scalia as a prime candidate for a Reagan nomination to the Supreme Court.

In March 1985, *The American Lawyer* profiled him as a "live wire" newcomer on the U.S. Circuit Court of Appeals for the District of Columbia, one of the busiest and for years most liberal appeals courts in the country.[6] Burger was a member of that court when he was named chief justice.

Scalia, 50, will be the first Supreme Court justice of Italian-American ancestry. He was born in Trenton, N.J., grew up in

---

[5] *Harvard Law Review*, Vol. 99/1; Vol. 98/1; Vol. 97/1; Vol. 92/1.
[6] *The American Lawyer*, March 1985.

A Crowded Docket Awaits
The Rehnquist Court

The Rehnquist court's first term will be a lively one, with 102 cases already set for argument, meaning the court's schedule already is filled well into February 1987.

Questions of First Amendment freedoms lead off the term as the Rehnquist court prepares to consider whether the Federal Election Commission (FEC) infringes the right of free speech by requiring Massachusetts Citizens for Life to set up a political action committee as the vehicle for its political expenditures.

In *Federal Election Commission v. Massachusetts Citizens for Life,* an appeals court said that when this requirement applies to "nonprofit, ideological" corporations like Massachusetts Citizens for Life, it infringes on their right of political speech. The FEC appealed, warning that exempting this sort of corporation would "open the way to the use of such corporations as a vehicle through which any corporation or union would be able to transform unlimited amounts of its treasury funds into political expenditures, while keeping the actual source of the financing secret."

Closed primary elections — in which only party members may vote — are at issue in a second First Amendment case, *Tashjian v. Republican Party of Connecticut.* Connecticut defends its right to require political parties to conduct such primaries. State Republicans have responded by arguing that such a law denies them their protected right of political association. Thirty-eight states have laws that could be affected by the court's ruling.

Although new Chief Justice William H. Rehnquist and new Justice Antonin Scalia both seem willing to accommodate religion in public life, the limits to which they will take that view will be tested when

the court hears *Edwards v. Aguillard.* Louisiana has protested a lower court ruling that it is unconstitutional for the legislature to require schools in which the theory of evolution is taught also to teach the competing theory of creationism, the biblically-based belief that God created the world.

Three times in the past six months, the court went out of its

way to spell out its continuing support of the general principle of affirmative action — the use of remedies based on race or sex to temporarily benefit a group that has suffered discrimination — even if certain affirmative action plans were found to run afoul of constitutional or legal prescriptions.*

Just a few days after the last of those decisions, the court put two more affirmative action cases on the docket, and these will provide Scalia with his first opportunity to address the issue of affirmative action from the bench.

In *United States v. Paradise,* the administration challenges as "plainly unconstitutional" an Alabama court-ordered affirmative action plan under which a black state trooper is promoted every time a white state trooper is promoted.

For the first time, in *Johnson v. Santa Clara County Transportation Agency,* the court will consider an affirmative action plan adopted to benefit women. In that case, a man who works for the transportation agency challenges the agency's promotion of a woman over him even though she scored two points lower on a qualifying exam.

The separation of powers, the basis for last term's decision that a key portion of the Gramm-Rudman-Hollings deficit reduction act was unconstitutional, is again before the court. *Burke v. Barnes* began as a challenge by several members of Congress to Reagan's use of a pocket veto to kill a bill while Congress was in recess between sessions.

As the case worked its way through the judicial system, a broader question emerged: Can members of Congress go to court to challenge a president's pocket veto?

In recent years, members of Congress have been increasingly disposed to go to court to challenge various executive branch actions. In this case, the administration wants the court to halt that trend. Its attorneys told the court: "Nothing in the role established for it by the Constitution confers on Congress a special right to ensure, outside of the political process, that its laws are enforced."

* *Wygant v. Jackson Board of Education; Local #28 of the Sheet Metal Workers' International v. Equal Employment Opportunity Commission; Local #93, International Association of Firefighters v. City of Cleveland.*

Antonin Scalia: a reputation for consensus-building.

Queens, N.Y., and is a Roman Catholic with nine children. A graduate of Georgetown University and Harvard Law School, he has practiced law in Cleveland, taught at the University of Virginia and University of Chicago law schools, and held several legal posts within the Nixon and Ford administrations, including that of head of the office of legal counsel from 1974-76, the job Rehnquist held from 1969-71.

In his writings on and off the bench, Scalia seems as congenial to the views of the Reagan administration as Rehnquist does. A key issue on which Scalia's personal views are in harmony with those of the Reagan administration is affirmative action, the notion that racial preferences may be used to temporarily favor members of a group that has previously suffered discrimination. Scalia and Reagan both view this as impermissible "reverse discrimination."

In other areas that are prominent on the Reagan social agenda, Scalia's religion and family background seem to justify the assumption that he opposes abortion and favors school prayer, though he has never made public his views on these issues.

Like Rehnquist, Scalia closely scrutinizes claims of constitutional rights and generally declines to expand their scope. When an activist group challenged administration regulations barring sleeping in Lafayette Park across from the White House, arguing that sleeping should be protected as part of their First Amendment freedom of expression, Scalia flatly rejected the idea that "sleeping is or ever can be speech for First Amendment purposes." [7]

Also like Rehnquist, Scalia argues for judicial restraint, contending that it is not the job of judges to create new rights or to expand existing ones. At the same time, however, Scalia has agreed with critics of judicial restraint that its advocates sometimes are more interested in results than in the principle.

[7] *Clark v. Community for Creative Non-Violence* (1984).

116

There may come a moment of truth, he has noted, when conservative critics of the courts have to decide "whether they really believe ... that the courts are doing too much, or whether they are actually nursing only the less principled grievance that the courts have not been doing what they want." [8]

Scalia, like Reagan, takes a strict view of the separation of powers, opposing experiments like the legislative veto that threaten the traditional separation of powers. He was, for example, one of the three judges voting last February to strike down a key provision of the Gramm-Rudman-Hollings Deficit Reduction Act as unconstitutional, a ruling upheld in July by the Supreme Court. [9]

Scalia's advocacy of free-market principles gives him the distinction of being the first modern economic conservative to sit on the Supreme Court. He believes that "the free market ... has historically been the cradle of broad political freedom, and in modern times the demise of economic freedom has been the grave of political freedom as well." [10]

However he votes, Scalia — a man of considerable personal charm and energy — is unlikely to vote alone. In four years on the appeals court, he has demonstrated his ability to build a consensus, quite an achievement on a court well-known for antagonistic relationships among its members.

Reagan's Campaign in Court

Reagan's hope for a conservative court is integral to his plan to lighten the hand of government in the lives of American citizens.

"It is no coincidence," he said in his first inaugural address, "that our present troubles parallel and are proportionate [to] the intervention and intrusion in our lives that have resulted from unnecessary and excessive growth of government."

From the beginning, the Reagan administration has argued that the Supreme Court should reconsider — and redirect — national policy on issues ranging from antitrust and abortion to

---

[8] Remarks made at the Cato Institute Conference on Economic Liberties and the Judiciary, Oct. 1984, and published under the title "On the Merits of the Frying Pan," in *Regulation*, AEI, Jan./Feb. 1985.

[9] *Bowsher v. Synar* (1986).

[10] Cato Institute Conference as quoted in the *Wall Street Journal*, "Judge Scalia Would Bring Reverence for Free Market to the Supreme Court," June 19, 1986.

questions of criminal law and the relationship between church and state.

These arguments had a common theme: they urged the court to relax the grip of government on individual decisions — those of businessmen, educators, employers and administrators. Only a few of these arguments have met a warm reception at the court, however, giving Rehnquist ample opportunity to dissent. Even some instances in which the administration appeared to prevail during Reagan's first term were subsequently turned into defeats when later cases were decided the other way during his second term.

Issues on which the the administration prevailed include its arguments in favor of permitting more public use of religious symbols, curtailing certain affirmative action plans and approving some exceptions to a controversial rule barring the use of illegally obtained evidence in criminal trials.[11]

Issues in which the court rebuffed the administration include its arguments in favor of granting tax-exempt status to private schools that discriminate against black students, of giving states more leeway to regulate abortions and of permitting regulatory agencies to rescind health and safety regulations.[12]

Two administration defeats — on abortion and school prayer — came in high-profile cases in which it pressed the court most aggressively. Such arguments seem to have had a particularly adverse effect on the key justices in the court's center. Both Powell and O'Connor voted against the administration on a 1985 school prayer case.[13]

Faceoff over Constitution's Original Intent

During the summer of 1985, in an unusually heated clash between the court and the executive branch the administration went public with its challenge to the court's reading of the Constitution. Attorney General Edwin Meese III delivered two scathing attacks, characterizing the court's decisions as "a jurisprudence of idiosyncracy" and urging its return to a more principled "jurisprudence of original intention."[14]

"The original meaning of constitutional provisions and statutes" is "the only reliable guide for judgment," Meese de-

---

[11] *Lynch v. Donnelly* (1984); *Firefighters Local Union #1784 v. Stotts* (1984); *United States v. Leon* (1984); *New York v. Quarles* (1984).
[12] *Bob Jones University v. U.S.* (1983); *Akron v. Akron Center for Reproductive Health* (1983); *Motor Vehicle Manufacturers Association v. State Farm Mutual Automobile Insurance Co.* (1983).
[13] *Thornburgh v. American College of Obstetricians and Gynecologists* (1986); *Wallace v. Jaffree* (1985).
[14] Speeches to the American Bar Association, July 9 and July 17, 1985. See "Constitutional Debate Renewed: Original Intent vs. Contemporary Contest," *E.R.R.*, Vol. I, No. 4, 1986.

clared. "Those who framed the Constitution chose their words carefully; they debated at great length the most minute points. The language they chose meant something. It is incumbent upon the court to determine what that meaning was."

A few months later, Justice William J. Brennan Jr. — the most senior and most liberal justice — responded. "We current Justices read the Constitution in the only way we can: as 20th-century Americans," he said. "The genius of the Constitution rests not in any static meaning it might have had in a world that is dead and gone, but in the adaptability of its great principles to cope with current problems and current needs. What the constitutional fundamentals meant to the wisdom of other times cannot be their measure to the vision of our time." [15]

If there were any doubt that the Reagan social agenda faced dim prospects in the Burger court, that uncertainty probably was dispelled last term, when the court handed down some stinging rebuffs to the administration.

On issues ranging from abortion to voting rights, the court underscored its continuing commitment to two liberal tenets that are anathema to the current occupants of the White House.

First, the court made clear that the government must continue to work actively to realize the goal of equality for all of its citizens. The administration has repeatedly declared that the nation has made enough progress toward a colorblind society and can abandon such remedial strategies as busing, racial quotas and hiring goals. In cases involving affirmative action, voting rights and jury selection, the court flatly refused to adopt that view.[16]

Second, the court upheld a continuing major role for federal courts in protecting and preserving individual rights. This was dramatically illustrated in decisions striking down federal regulations requiring hospitals to aggressively treat severely handicapped newborns, even over parental objections, and, in another case, reaffirming its view that government has little or no business interfering in a woman's right to have an abortion.[17]

"There is "a certain private sphere of individual liberty" that should "be kept largely beyond the reach of government," the court declared. The administration had urged the court to uphold the so-called "Baby Doe" regulations involving handicapped infants, and reverse itself to permit states free rein to regulate or ban abortions. Justices Rehnquist and O'Connor took the government's side in both cases.

[15] Speech at Georgetown University, Oct. 12, 1985.
[16] *Wygant v. Jackson Board of Education* (1986); *Thornburgh v. Gingles* (1986); *Batson v. Kentucky* (1986).
[17] *Brown v. American Hospital Association; Thornburgh v. American College of Obstetricians and Gynecologists.*

First Tests for Rehnquist Court

I n its busy first term, the Rehnquist court will address constitutional and statutory issues ranging from affirmative action to freedom of speech, from church and state to separation of powers. Speculating on the character of the new court, Howard of the University of Virginia said he expects a "sharpening of ideological divisions." He sees the court as becoming more divided into liberal and conservative camps with an end to the splintering and fragmentation that characterized the Burger court's response to many difficult issues it confronted.

Bruce Fein of AEI agrees. During the Burger era the court was "philosophically at sea," he said, but now the court will have at least two conservative members who will work to build a "philosophically consistent theme of jurisprudence."

.One of the most significant in-house powers Rehnquist will assume as chief justice is the power to assign the task of writing the court's opinion in a case. Having heard each justice state his or her views in conference, the chief justice can influence the shape of the precedent by selecting who will write the opinion, knowing already whether that justice views the ruling as narrow or expansive. However, the chief justice retains the power of assignment only if he is part of the majority. It is illustrative of the ideological divisions Howard foresees that on this court that power — when Rehnquist is in dissent — will pass to veteran justice Brennan, to the court's most systematic and outspoken liberal.

Will Scalia and Rehnquist Team Up?

If Rehnquist and Scalia become an effective team, Reagan's campaign for a conservative court will finally move from the courtroom to the conference room, where the justices argue the merits of cases and state their opinions. But the conservative campaign will succeed only if his appointees agree with each other — and can persuade at least some of the more moderate members of the court to go along.

There are certain traditions that could facilitate the development of this team — and would certainly enhance its effectiveness. As chief justice, Rehnquist will speak first on each case in conference. As the most junior justice, Scalia will vote first on each case. By thus bracketing the court's discussion, these two justices could have an impact far beyond their own two votes.

Frank describes as "vast" the power that a chief justice can wield as a result of setting the agenda and opening the discussion in conference. "Frequently the person who sets the agenda controls the meeting," Frank said. "The chief will be able to focus on the questions he wants to talk about; anyone who wants to talk about something else will have to disrupt that pattern."

Rehnquist and Scalia are the court's most committed conservatives. Brennan and Thurgood Marshall are equally consistent liberals. The balance of power on close questions is held by the remaining justices: O'Connor, White and Powell, who tend to — but don't always — take the conservative view of matters, and Harry A. Blackmun and John Paul Stevens, who tend to take the liberal view.

Howard predicts that the tempo of the debate will pick up, increasing the pressure on the justices in the middle to choose sides. "The argument on the conservative side will be more carefully worked out," he said, referring to Scalia's powerful legal intellect. "That will have a polarizing effect, attracting or repelling these other justices."

Where Will O'Connor Move Next?

The impact of that polarizing effect on O'Connor is significant and unpredictable. Rehnquist's promotion and Scalia's arrival come just as O'Connor seems to be shifting away from her steady alliance with Rehnquist toward a more centrist role on the court.

After four years of consistently voting with Burger and Rehnquist, O'Connor in 1986 made clear that she did not always agree with them. Such independence had been foreshadowed in June 1985, when she, with Powell, refused to go along with the administration's approval of the public school moment of silence law.[18]

The intensification of conservative arguments could drive O'Connor into a more frequent alliance with the liberals, Howard speculates, particularly on questions of religious freedom and sex discrimination, another issue on which she has consistently taken a more liberal stance than Rehnquist.

Although both have dissented from the court's recent rulings striking down state and local efforts to regulate abortion, O'Connor's stance on that issue differs from Rehnquist's. He is ready to overturn *Roe v. Wade* — the landmark 1973 decision that legalized abortion — and return control over this matter to the states, as the administration has urged. But O'Connor does not go so far, advocating instead that states be

---

[18] *Wallace v. Jaffree.*

Job Experience for Chief Justice May Not Mean Much

William H. Rehnquist, the 16th man to serve as chief justice of the Supreme Court, is the fourth to move up from associate justice. History suggests prior service may not be much of an indicator about performance in the court's top post.

Edward D. White *(top),* the first man to make the move up after being selected by President Taft in 1910, was not particularly distinguished in either post. He was, John P. Frank wrote in *Marble Palace* (Alfred A. Knopf, 1958) a simple and unpretentious man, "yet, while everyone liked White, no one ever supposed him to be an outstanding chief justice."

Chosen for the top job in 1940 by President Roosevelt, Harlan F. Stone *(bottom)* had served with notable distinction as an associate justice through the New Deal era when he became chief justice. But he was not very adept at leading the court. Frank recounted, although promotion "was accompanied by as nearly unanimous an accolade as ever occurs in our turbulent public life ... Stone was not a satisfactory chief justice.... A partisan battler himself, he could not rise above the fray to bring calm leadership into the controversies of others."

A much better performance was turned in by Charles Evans Hughes *(center),* who served six years as an associate justice, resigned to run unsuccessfully for president, and then spent 14 years as a distinguished attorney before being chosen by President Hoover in 1930 to return to the court as chief justice. "For all-around legal skill and superb administrative ability," wrote Frank, Hughes was the greatest chief justice since John Marshall.

The other chief justices were: John Jay, John Rutledge and Oliver Ellsworth, appointed by Washington; John Marshall, appointed by Adams; Roger B. Taney, named by Jackson; Salmon P. Chase, named by Lincoln; Morrison R. Waite, named by Grant; Melville W. Fuller, appointed by Cleveland; William Howard Taft, named by Harding; Fred M. Vinson, appointed by Truman; Earl Warren, appointed by Eisenhower; Warren Burger, appointed by Nixon.

given more leeway to regulate abortion as long as they do not "unduly burden" a woman's choice to terminate a pregnancy.[19]

O'Connor went out of her way in May, when the court held a particular affirmative action plan unconstitutional, to point out that the majority agreed that some such plans were indeed permissible to remedy job bias. And she split with Rehnquist to join the majority in two libel rulings, each of which were hailed as major victories for the press.[20]

Would Powell Swing to Conservatives?

O'Connor's move toward the center has aligned her with Powell, who throughout nearly 15 years on the court, has maintained just enough independence from a conservative label to wield considerable power when the court is divided closely on an issue.

No better example of his pivotal vote can be found than the court's much discussed sodomy ruling last June. By a 5-4 vote — with Powell and O'Connor in the majority — the court upheld a state law criminalizing sodomy.[21]

Soon after the ruling, *The Washington Post* reported that Powell had been the key vote — that he had first voted to strike the law down and then had changed his vote to uphold it. Powell acknowledged that this was the case, emphasizing that the man bringing the case had not in fact been prosecuted. Powell made clear in his concurring opinion that he would not vote to uphold such laws if they were used to justify severe punishment for such activity.[22]

If Scalia can use his considerable talents of intellectual and personal persuasion to swing Powell and O'Connor firmly into the conservative wing of the court, only one more vote would be needed to secure conservative dominance in decision-making on a variety of issues.

Observers think such a swing could happen, particularly if Rehnquist and Scalia forge a good working relationship. Fein thinks they will work "splendidly together," noting that both are congenial, unpretentious men who enjoy good rapport with their colleagues.

"It could be quite a team," said Howard, "with one assigning the opinions, and the other employing as powerful a mind as the court will have."

---

[19] *Thornburgh v. American College of Obstetricians and Gynecologists.*
[20] *Wygant v. Jackson Board of Education; Liberty Lobby v. Anderson; Hepps v. Philadelphia Newspapers Inc.*
[21] *Bowers v. Hardwick.* The Georgia law which was upheld banned sodomy between consenting adults, regardless of sexual orientation, but the majority opinion made clear that the Constitution did not protect homosexual conduct per se.
[22] *The Washington Post,* July 13, 1986.

Recommended Reading List

Books

Frank, John P., *Marble Palace*, Alfred A. Knopf, 1958.

Hughes, Charles Evans, *The Supreme Court of the United States*, Columbia University Press, 1928.

O'Brien, David M., *Storm Center: The Supreme Court in American Politics*, W. W. Norton & Co., 1986.

Swindler, William F., *Court and Constitution in the 20th Century: The New Legality, 1932-1968*, Bobbs-Merrill Co., 1970.

Tribe, Laurence, *Constitutional Choices*, Harvard University Press, 1985.

——, *God Save This Honorable Court*, Random House, 1985.

Witt, Elder, *A Different Justice*, Congressional Quarterly Inc., 1986.

——, ed., *Guide to the U.S. Supreme Court*, Congressional Quarterly Inc., 1979.

Articles

Adler, Stephen J., "Live Wire on the D.C. Circuit," *The American Lawyer*, March 1985.

Danelski, David J., "The Influence of the Chief Justice in the Decisional Process of the Supreme Court," included in *American Court Systems*, Sheldon Goldman and Austin Sarat, eds., W. H. Freeman & Co., 1978.

Fein, Bruce, "High Court Upheaval Presages Conservative Shift," *The Legal Times*, June 23, 1986.

Reports

Editorial Research Reports: "Constitutional Debate Renewed," 1986 Vol. I, p. 63; "The Modern First Amendment," 1985 Vol. I, p. 1; "Balancing Church and State," 1984 Vol. II, p. 917; "Television in the Courtroom," 1981 Vol. I, p. 19.

Graphics: P. 105 photo, Joseph McCary, Photo Response; photo p. 107, Ken Heinen; photos p. 110, World Wide Photos, Ken Heinen, Sue Klemens and Joseph McCary, Photo Response; photo p. 115, Teresa Zabala; photos p. 116, Joseph McCary, Photo Response.

WESTERN

WATER

by

Tom Arrandale

Jan. 30
1 9 8 7

Sunbelt's Urban Thirst

Water is growing more precious than ever in the American West. Sun Belt cities, worried about serving expanding populations and attracting new industries, are searching far and near for future water reserves. Farmers and ranchers, Indian tribes, federal land agencies and environmental groups are protecting their rights or pressing new claims to the rivers and underground streams. The era of reclaiming the deserts is fading, and the vast arid regions of the West now are adjusting to the natural limits of water supplies. Much of the available water in the West has become a marketable commodity.

"The West is beginning to feel the desert winds of reality," Richard D. Lamm, the former governor of Colorado, has declared.[1] Agriculture's long domination of western water resources is yielding, however slowly, to the growing political clout of the Sun Belt's super cities, whose future growth is jeopardized for want of adequate water supplies. It is in the metropolitan areas, not in the wide-open spaces of folklore, that the western population is concentrated. The urban demand for a greater share of the available water addresses still another reality. It is that the federal government's past generosity in funding new water projects is evaporating.

Past Decade's Change in Political Climate

A decade ago, President Carter fanned the "winds of reality" by trying to cancel 19 of the 320 water projects then being federally funded, including several that western states had counted on to tap what they considered their fair share of the few rivers within reach. Sending this list to Congress in a revision of his predecessor's budget was one of Carter's first acts. Though he achieved a partial victory, it was politically costly. Several senior lawmakers from affected states denounced his "hit list," souring his relations with Congress and initially reinforcing the notion that a politician could cripple water projects only at his peril.[2]

During the following 10 years, however, political support for water-supply projects has been eroded by federal budget deficits, environmental concerns and economic analyses. In Congress, an alliance between environmental groups and fiscal conservatives demanded that the government stop financing

---

[1] Richard D. Lamm, "A New Era in Western Water Policy," *American Water Works Association Journal*, October 1986, p. 12. Lamb, a Democrat who left office Jan. 13, 1987, has written and spoken extensively on regional and national problems relating to the exhaustion and misuse of natural resources. The American Water Works Association is a Denver-based trade group composed primarily of officials of municipal water agencies and private supply industries.
[2] The revised budget was submitted to Congress Feb. 22, 1977. Eventually, funding was removed from nine projects. See Congressional Quarterly's *1977 Almanac*, pp. 650-58.

new water developments that destroy river ecosystems and subsidize wasteful irrigation practices.

James G. Watt, President Reagan's first Interior secretary, took office in 1981 pledging to start new projects. But congressional action was delayed several more years by debate within the administration over cost-sharing proposals to force state and local governments to pay part of the government's up-front costs in building water facilities.

Finally last October, Congress cleared legislation granting the U.S. Army Corps of Engineers authority to undertake 260 new dam and harbor projects that demand higher cost-sharing by the beneficiaries. But this year's construction budget for the U.S. Bureau of Reclamation, the Interior Department agency that has built and operated most federally financed water developments in the 17 westernmost states *(see map, p. 134)*, is only marginally above the one that Watt inherited in 1981.[3]

New Federal 'Hit List' of Water Projects

Reagan, in his new budget for fiscal 1988, has offered what amounts to his own "hit list" of western water projects. As announced Jan. 9 by Wayne Marchant, acting assistant Interior secretary, the administration wants to "zero out" — in effect eliminate — funding for all but 12 of the 50 water projects being planned by the Bureau of Reclamation. At the same time, 15 projects that are under way would receive added funding to bring them to completion faster so that the government could start collecting fees sooner from the water users.

In response to the events of the past decade, westerners show signs that they are starting to learn to live with long-term water scarcities. In 1980, Arizona adopted a comprehensive groundwater code in an effort to halt the rapid depletion of aquifers that provide water for fast-growing Phoenix and Tucson. In 1982, California voters rejected building still another canal to carry water from the state's northern rivers to Southern California. No longer counting on federal dam-building programs to provide new supplies, state and city officials are promoting water-saving campaigns and buying up farmlands to acquire their water rights for the benefit of urban homes and factories.

Throughout the West, state engineers and water departments now assume that the region must meet future needs by transferring water from agriculture to fast-growing cities. Yet many farmers, whose families have spent decades trying to subdue

---

[3] The bureau's budget authority for construction in 1981 was $576 million; the 1987 budget is $602 million. For 1988, the Reagan administration's budget request is $700 million.

western deserts, are still reluctant to part with water rights that give their lands value. "Controlling your share of water has clearly been the key, not just to survival, but to economic growth and prosperity," notes John A. Folk-Williams, who has written extensively about water law. "There is a deep-seated fear about cities or speculators coming in and taking effective control over a community by taking control of its water." [4] But recent court decisions and economic trends may be breaking down western water-law doctrines that discourage farmers from conserving water and selling their surplus to urban users.

Water Quality at Issue Across the Nation

If new dam-building is losing favor nationally, the same cannot be said for federal spending to reduce stream pollution and assure safe drinking water. This became abundantly evident when the new 100th Congress, in its first major action, promptly passed a bill identical to one that President Reagan pocket-vetoed last November for extending the Clean Water Act of 1972. He objected that spending some $18 billion over eight years, as the bill authorized, was fiscally unsound in a time of budget reductions. Nevertheless, when the second round of voting came in January, the bill received overwhelming approval in both houses,[5] and by lawmakers from both parties, reflecting a national awareness that pollution of streams and underground water supplies threatens the purity of the drinking water in many places.

While water quality has been at issue at least since the 1960s, most non-westerners continued to assume water supplies were ample. But within the past two years, other Americans have been reminded that no part of the country can be assured of water at all times. In the spring of 1985, several eastern states declared a drought emergency and asked residents to cut back non-essential uses. Many cities in the Northeast and Midwest must cope with inadequate reservoirs and leaking water delivery systems. Even booming Florida, with an average annual rainfall of 53 inches — 23 more than the national average — has been struggling to reverse the destruction of environmentally sensitive wetlands and falling groundwater tables that supply most of its needs.[6] Last summer a devastating drought spread over wide areas of the normally humid South and into the Middle Atlantic states.

Despite such warning signs, Americans continue to waste tremendous amounts of water. For most of the nation's history,

---

[4] Telephone interview, December 1986. Folk-Williams is president of Western Network, a non-profit foundation in Santa Fe, N.M., engaged in water studies.
[5] The House of Representatives passed the bill by a 406-9 vote Jan. 6 and the Senate by a 93-6 vote Jan. 21, 1987. For a review of earlier concerns about water purity, see "Drinking Water Safety," *E.R.R.*, 1974 Vol. I, pp. 121-40.
[6] See "America's Disappearing Wetlands," *E.R.R.*, 1983 Vol. II, pp. 613-32.

federal, state and local governments have pursued policies aimed at developing new water supplies — by building dams, reservoirs and diversion canals to store water and transport it where it was needed. Those efforts have kept water rates so low that consumers have little economic incentive to limit use. In an American household equipped with lawn sprinklers, flush toilets and dishwashers, the per-person use may run to more than 250 gallons a day.

On average, the U.S. Geological Survey reports, the national water consumption — personal, industrial and agricultural — exceeds 100 billion gallons a day, which is only 1/14th of the potential supply. Unfortunately for many westerners, the nation's supply is uneven, as is indicated on the rainfall distribution map. *(See p. 134).* There are geologists and historians who insist that the true West begins at the 100th meridian, the line of longitude that runs north-south from the Dakotas down through the Texas Panhandle. From about that line westward to the Pacific coastal mountain ranges, most of the land receives an average annual rainfall of less than 20 inches — enough to nourish sparse vegetation for livestock grazing but not for tilling the soil without irrigation.

Some of the land receives far less than 20 inches and is true desert, a label that map-makers applied to the entire region in the early 19th century. Walter Prescott Webb, the late University of Texas historian, spoke of the 20th century West as an "oasis civilization," in which big cities grow up amid vast, largely uninhabited deserts and plains.[7]

Instead of trying to expand supplies, conservationists and economists long have argued that the nation should let water prices rise to levels that would limit use by encouraging conservation. In 1978, President Carter proposed a national water policy to link future water-project construction with conservation, water-quality protection, and long-term planning to balance supply and demand. Congress ignored his proposal, and the Reagan administration disbanded the federal Water Resources Council, an advisory body that had been pushing for more efficient water use as an alternative to dam construction.

End of Reclamation Era

But the arid West no longer seems able to postpone a reckoning with the limits of its water supplies. For a century, western states have prospered and grown by diverting rivers and

[7] For background, see "Western Water: Coming Crisis," *E.R.R.*, 1977 Vol. I, pp. 31-32.

drilling deep wells to irrigate crops and supply water to city dwellers. Ever since Congress passed the Reclamation Act of 1902, the federal government has been damming western rivers to generate electric power and deliver low-cost water to farmers and fast-growing metropolitan areas.

The great rivers that drain the West have already been dammed at the most practical sites. And the West cannot rely much longer on uncontrolled pumping from underground aquifers. Since World War II, farmers and urban developers have been "mining" groundwater from beneath Arizona deserts surrounding Phoenix and Tucson and the Ogallala Aquifer beneath the High Plains from Nebraska south into the Texas Panhandle. These withdrawals are rapidly draining away water that has been deposited there for thousands of years.

Plans that were advanced a decade ago to augment western water supplies by seeding clouds or desalting brackish water no longer seem practical. Rising construction costs and opposition from other regions have ended dreams of diverting water to the Southwest from the Columbia River Basin or the Mississippi Valley. And rising congressional opposition to new projects indicates that those now being built may be the last.

The big works under construction include several units of the Upper Colorado River Basin Storage Project, approved by Congress in 1956 to enable Colorado, New Mexico, Wyoming, and Utah to develop their shares of Colorado River system water allocated by an interstate compact in 1922. The Central Arizona Project, a controversial system that Congress authorized in 1968, last year began pumping water 190 miles from the Colorado River to Phoenix. The water delivery is scheduled to reach Tucson by 1991.

Another large undertaking is the Central Utah Project, which will carry water across Utah's Wasatch Mountains to Salt Lake City and surrounding cities. But the Reagan administration's cost-sharing demands are making some long-planned projects more expensive to the users. Utah voters approved a higher repayment rate to reimburse federal construction costs for the Central Utah Project, and New Mexico and Colorado recently agreed to pick up part of the costs of building the Animas-LaPlata Project in the Four Corners region where those states meet with Arizona and Utah. But while western states may be able to finance some small water diversions, "It's really hard to justify a lot of these projects from an economic standpoint," said Steven J. Shupe of Santa Fe, N.M., a specialist in water-rights law — a "water lawyer" as his breed is known in the West.[8]

---

[8] Interview, December 1986.

When first conceived in the 1940s, both the Arizona and Utah projects were intended primarily to provide irrigation water. But when completed, both will supply water to metropolitan centers that have spread in the past 40 years across surrounding farmlands. Out on the High Plains of Texas, rising energy costs and falling water tables in the Ogallala Aquifer are forcing farmers to turn off their pumps and return to dryland farming, with its lower per-acre crop yields and greater vulnerability to drought. In Arizona, the 1980 groundwater law provides a mechanism for retiring land from cultivation and converting irrigation rights to municipal use. Irrigated acreage has declined steadily in the West since 1979, and the bleak profit outlook for American farmers is expected to accelerate the trend.

Extensive Reach by Fast-Growing Cities

Agriculture still uses roughly 90 percent of the water that the West consumes. Yet for all its fabled open spaces, the West since World War II has — in one sense — become the most urbanized region in the country. In the vast distances between sizable cities, the countryside supports relatively few people. Job-seekers from Mexico and job-and-sun-seekers from elsewhere in the United States flock to the few large metropolitan areas of the American Southwest, primarily to Los Angeles, San Diego, Phoenix, Tucson, Denver, Salt Lake City, El Paso and Albuquerque. On average, three of every four people in the western Sun Belt live in metropolitan areas; in California, 95 percent do.

Because the climate is so dry, residential water use in the western communities averages 50 percent more than in eastern regions. Air conditioning and evaporative "swamp coolers" have become standard equipment in southwestern homes and buildings to make desert summers more comfortable. Newcomers from more humid regions have planted trees, bluegrass, and other water-consuming plants around homes, parks, golf courses, and other urban facilities. More than half of the water that Denver uses is for lawns.

Most western cities long ago outgrew local water supplies and began reaching out to tap faraway rivers or deep underground reservoirs. Los Angeles in 1913 started siphoning water 230 miles from Owens Valley on the far side of the Sierra Nevada range. Congress approved federal construction of Hoover Dam and other structures across the Colorado River, in part to supply Los Angeles with enough added water and power to support its rapid expansion. Since 1940, the water has flowed to the Los Angeles area through a 242-mile-long aqueduct. San Diego tapped into that system in 1947. This flow has since been supplemented by water carried through streams and canals

A WATER VIEW
OF THE WEST

Annual | 0-10
Inches of | 10-20
Rainfall | over 20

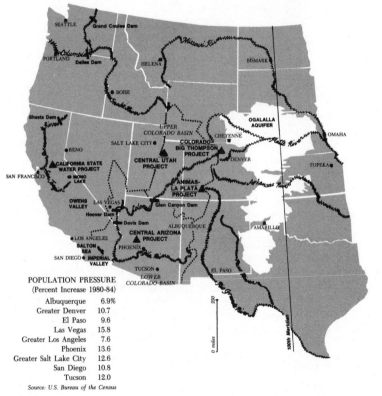

SEATTLE
Grand Coulee Dam
Columbia
PORTLAND
Dalles Dam
HELENA
BISMARK
Missouri River
BOISE
Shasta Dam
OGALALLA
AQUIFER
UPPER
COLORADO BASIN
SALT LAKE CITY
COLORADO
BIG THOMPSON
PROJECT
CHEYENNE
OMAHA
RENO
Platte River
CALIFORNIA STATE
WATER PROJECT
CENTRAL UTAH
PROJECT
DENVER
TOPEKA
SAN FRANCISCO
MONO
LAKE
ANIMAS-
LA PLATA
PROJECT
Arkansas River
OWENS
VALLEY
LAS VEGAS
Glen Canyon Dam
Hoover Dam
Colorado
Davis Dam
ALBUQUERQUE
AMARILLO
LOS ANGELES
SALTON
SEA
CENTRAL ARIZONA
PROJECT
SAN DIEGO
IMPERIAL
VALLEY
PHOENIX
TUCSON
LOWER
COLORADO BASIN
EL PASO
100th Meridian

POPULATION PRESSURE
(Percent Increase 1980-84)

Albuquerque	6.9%
Greater Denver	10.7
El Paso	9.6
Las Vegas	15.8
Greater Los Angeles	7.6
Phoenix	13.6
Greater Salt Lake City	12.6
San Diego	10.8
Tucson	12.0

Source: U.S. Bureau of the Census

0 miles   350

from northern California by the state-built California State Water Project.

Denver acquired much of its water supply by pumping water from the Colorado River headwaters through tunnels bored beneath the front range of the Rocky Mountains. Upper Colorado River Basin projects are enlarging the water supplies of Utah's cities, Albuquerque, and smaller communities in New Mexico and also Colorado. Phoenix for years has taken part of its supply from Salt River dams, and the Central Arizona Project water will let both Phoenix and Tucson curtail their reliance on declining groundwater reserves.

The pace of the West's urban growth has slowed since the energy boom of the 1970s collapsed. Nevertheless, Denver's current water supplies cannot support some projections of population growth much beyond 1990. Tucson, the largest American city that depends completely on groundwater, for years has been alarmed by falling water tables. El Paso relies heavily on dwindling groundwater reserves. Reno, Nev., depends primarily on the little Truckee River. In Southern California, the Metropolitan Water District looks for a population growth of four million in this decade and the next. This comes at a time when Arizona, under terms of a 1963 Supreme Court ruling, *Arizona v. California,* is beginning to divert some of the Colorado River water that Southern California has been using.

Meanwhile, farmers and environmentalists are challenging Los Angeles' right to pump groundwater from Owens Valley and, farther north, from Mono Lake. If those diversions are curtailed, San Diego might lose some of its 25 percent share of the Metropolitan Water District; Los Angeles could exercise superior rights to the district's supplies. In 1982, California voters defeated a ballot proposal to build the Peripheral Canal, to augment State Water Project supplies and partly offset losses of Colorado River water to Arizona. The canal project was defeated by the heavy opposition of Northern California residents who resent Southern California's thirst for their water.

Region's 'Water Politics' and Novel Law

Ever since frontier days, the struggle to find water and put it to use has directed the West's economic course and driven its political life. Just as racial issues once dominated the South, "the West also comes close to practicing single-issue politics — in its case, the politics of water," said Ed Marston, who writes often about regional issues in the biweekly newspaper *High Country News,* which he publishes at Paonia, Colo.[9]

---

[9] Ed Marston, "Western Water Made Simple," *High Country News,* Sept. 29, 1986.

Western water politics have set farmers against townspeople, state against state, region against region, and more recently environmentalists against federal dam-construction agencies. Pioneer ranchers established control over vast stretches of land by staking claim to crucial rivers and springs. In the early decades of this century, Los Angeles assured itself of water needed for growth by secretively buying up farmlands at bargain prices in California's distant Owens Valley. Arizona called out its National Guard in 1933 to halt work on projects diverting water from the Colorado River on its border for a pipeline to Los Angeles.

But after decades of bitter wrangling, state governments worked out a series of interstate compacts for sharing the waters of the major western rivers. By taking a unified stand in Washington, trading off support for projects to develop each state's share, powerful congressional delegations pushed through federal dam-building programs that made it possible to put the rivers to use.

Over the course of a century, western water rivalries have produced unique legal arrangements for allocating scarce water to economic use. In eastern states, where governments adopted the "riparian law" doctrine that evolved in well-watered England, the owners of land along a stream's banks share rights to use its water. But in the West, where streams are widely separated and often run dry part of the year, 19th century settlers developed new procedures for allocating water too scarce to go around.

Miners in California's gold fields agreed that the prospectors who first diverted water from a stream to work a claim thereby established a superior water right. Later, when the farmers came, they accepted the same principle, the doctrine of prior appropriation. Those who first tapped the streams to irrigate their fields or put the water to other, generally unspecified "beneficial" uses, gained senior rights to it. This doctrine enabled them to take everything and leave other users without water in times of shortages. Following this doctrine, state governments set up processes under which state engineers, water commissioners, or special water courts settle water conflicts, approve water right transfers, and make sure that changes in water diversion will not cut supplies to senior users.[10]

The fear of losing out spurred westerners to start developing their rivers as quickly as possible — before neighbors, nearby communities, or even other states could establish prior beneficial use. Lacking capital to build their own big dams and

---

[10] California, Idaho, Washington and Oregon, states that have both dry and well-watered areas, retain features of riparian law in their water allocation systems.

irrigation canals, westerners turned to the federal government. In the Reclamation Act of 1902, Congress authorized the Bureau of Reclamation to finance, build, and operate huge storage projects along the Colorado, Missouri, Columbia, Rio Grande and tributary streams.

Farmers Fight to Retain Water Subsidies

In theory, western farmers would use federal project water to irrigate 160-acre homesteads, repaying the government for its costs.[11] In practice, water project beneficiaries ignored the 160-acre limit. To halt a drive by environmentalists and land-reform advocates to deny low-cost water to wealthy individuals and corporations that irrigated thousands of acres, Congress in 1982 raised the official limit to 960 acres but applied full charges on water delivery for most additional acreage. The users were given five years, until April 12, 1987, to renegotiate their irrigation contracts. Some, mostly in California, have not done so, and have challenged the new provisions in a series of lawsuits. If there is no new contract by the deadline, the user in most circumstances must pay full cost for the irrigation of more than 160 acres.

Subsidies vary from project to project. For the bureau's Central Valley Project in California, for instance, beneficiaries had repaid only $50 million of the total $931 million cost in 40 years, according to a 1983 study. It added that the prevailing charge was $6.15 per acre foot — the amount of water needed to cover an acre of land to a depth of one foot — while the actual cost was $72.99.

As federal projects were being designed and built, state governments empowered farmers receiving the water to form quasi-governmental irrigation or "conservancy" districts to manage the distribution system. With taxing authority and power to regulate water transfers, the districts developed into influential political bases throughout the rural West. Along with state legislatures that often were dominated by ranchers and farmers, the districts have been formidable advocates of developing western water resources.

The requirement that water be put to "beneficial use" has never been interpreted as demanding the most efficient practices. Waste is encouraged by a "use it or lose it" dictum requiring that water be continuously diverted to maintain legal rights to it. California revised its water code in 1982 to permit water saved through conservation to be "sold, leased, exchanged, or otherwise transferred." Other states have not followed California's lead, however, and some critics charge that western farmers could reap huge profits by selling low-cost

---

[11] For background, see "Western Land Policy," *E.R.R.*, 1978 Vol. I, pp. 86-89.

water from federally subsidized projects to city and industrial users willing to pay much higher prices.

Throughout the West's development, it has been common practice to buy up land simply to acquire water rights that go with it. Subject to many restrictions, state water laws allow water rights to be sold and transferred to different uses. But irrigation districts, trying to protect their tax base and crop production, often prohibit transfer of water beyond existing water project boundaries. Bureau of Reclamation regulations for some western projects also bar water transfers from agricultural uses. Western state governments have in addition sought to prohibit the export of water beyond their boundaries.

Farm-to-City Transfer

As the West's urban growth accelerates, changing economic and political conditions are starting to break down the old water-allocation arrangements. This growth since World War II has created industrial and municipal demands for water that could yield far greater returns than irrigated agriculture. Cities and corporations can afford to pay far more for water than can farmers. And city governments and municipal water departments, trying to fill projected needs for 50 to 100 years to come, in recent years have launched aggressive and innovative drives to secure rights to future supplies.

With the economic power that accompanies rapid industrial growth, cities are bidding high prices to buy up farmlands and irrigation water rights. With their voter rolls reflecting increased populations, western cities are steadily displacing agriculture and mining as the West's predominant political forces. "Major cities not only have the financial ability to purchase large quantities of water . . . , but also often have the political power to change legislatively the institutional mechanisms for managing the resource," a 1985 study of western urban water needs concluded.[12]

Water: Market Commodity in the Rockies

As a result, water is becoming a market commodity in the West. During a 1976-77 drought, several short-term trades took place between the Los Angeles Metropolitan Water District, which had surplus Colorado River supplies, and other hard-

[12] John A. Folk-Williams, Susan C. Fry and Lucy Hilgendorf, *Western Water Flows to the Cities*, Western Network, 1985, p. 4.

pressed regions. Phoenix, Tucson and their suburbs have been engaging in "water ranching" — a practice of buying up rangeland to acquire its water. Greeley, Colo., has contracted with farmers for rights to call on their irrigation water in case of drought; Casper, Wyo., has started financing conservation measures for farmers to make salvaged water available for urban use. In northern Colorado, the trading of water rights became so active that "water brokers" went into business, listing bids and offers for water from the Colorado-Big Thompson project.

In California's fertile Central Valley, corporate farming operations have approached San Diego and the Metropolitan Water District about selling water rights. Meanwhile, court cases and development planners are testing whether state governments and interstate compacts can legally restrict water rights transactions that would move water across state lines.

In a 1982 decision, *Sporhase v. Nebraska*, the Supreme Court declared water a commodity that falls under the Constitution's commerce clause, which forbids restrictions on interstate commerce. The decision prohibited states from arbitrarily barring the passage of their water across state lines. El Paso, Texas, seeking groundwater supplies in New Mexico, is challenging a New Mexico law, revised after the Sporhase decision, that directs the state engineer to consider the impact of an interstate water transfer on the health and safety of New Mexico residents before he approves it.

San Diego, worried about future supplies after defeat of the Peripheral Canal proposal in 1982, acquired an option to buy Upper Colorado River Basin water from a private Colorado company. That firm, the Galloway Group, holds senior water rights on the Yampa River, a Colorado tributary, on which it proposes to build a dam near Meeker, Colo. The proposal is encountering opposition from Arizona, Upper Basin states and Los Angeles, where officials fear the precedent could undermine arrangements of the Colorado River compact.

Conservation in California, on the Plains

In California, a water transaction is now being discussed that could test the prospects for saving once-wasted irrigation water and making it available to cities. Two years ago, the California Water Resources Control Board ruled that the Imperial Irrigation District, which supplies Colorado River water to farmers in the Imperial Valley, was violating a state constitution prohibition on wasting water. The board found that the irrigation district, which receives nearly 3 million acre feet of the river's 14 million acre feet of flow each year, was wasting nearly a million acre feet by allowing water to seep from fields, unlined ditches, and spilling canals.

WHO USES WESTERN WATER?

Although irrigated acreage in the arid West has declined in recent years and growing cities are seeking out more water, the overwhelming use of western water resources is agricultural. Here is the breakdown for seven states.

AGRICULTURE

	Irrigated Acres, 1984	Percent of Total Cropland	Percent State Water Use, 1980
ARIZONA	893,200	60%	89%
CALIFORNIA	7,805,100	69	92
COLORADO	3,104,900	29	90
NEVADA	698,500	81	88
NEW MEXICO	674,400	30	89
TEXAS	4,921,400	13	80
UTAH	1,053,600	55	83

MUNICIPALITIES

	Million Gallons Used Daily, 1980	Percent State Water Use, 1980
ARIZONA	340	8%
CALIFORNIA	1,700	7
COLORADO	160	4
NEVADA	69	4
NEW MEXICO	99	5
TEXAS	640	6
UTAH	300	10

Sources: U.S. Bureau of the Census and U.S. Geographical Survey

Following up on a plan advanced by the Environmental Defense Fund, a national environmental organization, Southern California, looking for water to replace Colorado River diversions by the Central Arizona Project, stepped in with a proposal to finance $10 million a year in studies and conservation investments for the irrigation district. In return, it would receive rights to use 100,000 acre feet of salvaged water for the Los Angeles area. Negotiations broke off in the summer of 1986 as opposition mounted among Imperial farmers. However, the idea remains alive. Economic and political pressures for a trade continue to build up.

Western state governments are starting to promote conservation. With the High Plains farming economy threatened by the Ogallala Aquifer's steady depletion, Texas Commissioner of Agriculture Jim Hightower has pushed for state subsidies to help farmers pay for water-conserving irrigation equipment. Arizona's innovative 1980 Groundwater Management Act requires that areas with dwindling groundwater reserves bring usage down to the level of replenishment by the year 2025. The law was passed after Cecil D. Andrus, President Carter's Interior secretary, threatened to withhold Central Arizona Project funding until the state dealt with groundwater depletion. The Arizona law taxes groundwater pumping, bans the irrigation of new lands, and empowers the state to start buying and retiring farmland in the year 2006 if necessary to meet the 2025 goal.

While the potential for saving water is highest in agriculture, western cities are starting to promote conservation. Tucson has cut water consumption 20 percent over five years through stiff water rate increases and other measures. El Paso, facing severe long-term shortages, has cut groundwater pumping through conservation drives and by substituting more expensive surface supplies from the Rio Grande. State and city officials in California, Colorado and Texas have been urging homeowners to replace grass lawns with native desert vegetation. California leads the nation in municipal wastewater reclamation.[13]

Indian Claims Clouding the Future Supply

Even as water starts flowing from farms to cities, the future allocation of water in the West remains clouded by potentially huge Indian claims to water for their reservations. In a 1908 decision, *Winters v. U.S.*, the Supreme Court ruled that Congress, when it created Indian reservations, implicitly gave tribes a right to the water they needed. Nearly 80 years later, the amount of water that the Winters doctrine confers on more than 200 western reservations has yet to be determined.

---

[13] See Sandra Postel's, *Conserving Water: The Untapped Alternative,* Worldwatch Institute, September 1985.

In a 1984 report for the Western Governors Association, the Salt Lake City-based Western States Water Council compiled estimates suggesting that Indian water rights across the West could surpass 45 million acre feet a year, more than three times the Colorado's annual flow.[14] The Western Conference of the Council of State Governments has called for federal legislation to give the tribes eight years to start using or lose their Winters rights.

Many reservations may lack sufficient population or lands suitable for irrigation, but tribal leaders might find it attractive to sell water to off-reservation cities or industries. As part of a settlement of competing groundwater claims near Tucson, Congress authorized Arizona's Papago tribe to sell or lease its share to other users. Montana has set up a commission to negotiate water rights settlements with its tribes; a 1985 compact with the Fort Peck reservation permits the leasing of tribal water from the Missouri River system.

Environmentalist Factor in Water Politics

Conflicting claims to the West's rivers and streams already far exceed the amount of water that flows down them. Even as those demands are sorted out, westerners are starting to recognize that water may be most valuable when left in place to nurture their region's wildlife and scenic regions. With both mining and agriculture fading as economic mainstays, western states are growing more dependent on tourists attracted by mountain and desert splendors. Newcomers drawn by the West's beauty and outdoor recreation opportunities are strengthening environmental groups that oppose new water projects that block clear-running streams and drown remote rock-walled canyons.

In some states, environmental groups have made themselves major players in western water politics. They oppose new dams, on economic as well as ecological grounds, pressing instead for higher water rates and incentives for conservation. In the Denver area, an environmental movement that took hold in the 1970s has been questioning new water treatment plants and reservoirs. Environmentalists now are challenging the Denver Water Board's plan to build a fourth dam on the South Platte River in the mountains west of Denver. The proposed Two Forks Dam would flood one of Colorado's finest remaining trout streams and disrupt the habitat of the Pawnee mountain skipper, a rare butterfly whose range is confined to the South Platte Canyon.[15]

---

[14] Western Governors' Association, "Indian Water Rights in the West," May 1984.
[15] See Alex Shoumatoff, "The Skipper and the Dam," *The New Yorker,* Dec. 1, 1986, p. 71.

Under pressure from Pacific Northwest Indian tribes and commercial fishermen, Congress has directed federal agencies to manage water releases by a series of dams on the Columbia River system to preserve the river's salmon fishery as well as generate electric power. The West's increasingly influential recreation industry, including ski resorts, whitewater rafting firms, and hunting and fishing equipment suppliers, sometimes joins in pressing for stream protection.

In other ways, too, state water laws and doctrines are being changed to accommodate the public interest in water issues. Montana in 1985 revised its water laws to tighten state controls over large diversions. And in a 1983 ruling in a lawsuit brought by the National Audubon Society, the California Supreme Court declared that Los Angeles' water diversions that were lowering the level of Mono Lake in northern California should be curtailed to protect the public's interest in preserving the lake's fragile ecosystem. For the first time, the Mono Lake ruling applied to inland waters the Public Trust Doctrine, an ancient English legal concept limiting private actions that impinged on public interests in using coastal waters.[16]

Although the federal government is now withdrawing from its historic role in developing western water resources, it will continue to manage the huge dam and canal systems it has created. The government also exerts its influence as the biggest landowner in the West. Just as Congress established water rights for Indian reservations, courts have ruled that the government controls reserved rights to water for national parks, forests, wildlife refuges, and other federal lands set aside from the public domain. A district court has upheld a Sierra Club lawsuit contending that Congress reserves water rights to maintain wilderness values when it designates federal wilderness areas. From many directions has come the change that is being wrought in the way the West deals with its growing thirst for water.

[16] For a discussion of the decision, see Charles F. Wilkinson's "Western Water Law in Transition," *American Water Works Association Journal*, October 1986, p. 44.

Recommended Reading List

Books

Portney, Paul R., ed., *Current Issues in National Resource Policy,* Resources for the Future Inc., Johns Hopkins University Press, 1982.

Powledge, Fred, *Water, The Nature, Uses, and Future of Our Most Precious and Abused Resource,* Farrar, Straus, Giroux, 1982.

Reisner, Marc, *Cadillac Desert, The American West and Its Disappearing Water,* Viking Penguin Inc., 1986.

Articles

Shupe, Steven J., "Emerging Forces in Western Water Law," *Resource Law Notes,* University of Colorado Natural Resources Law Center, April 1986, p. 2.

"Water Law in the West," *American Water Works Association Journal,* October 1986.

"Western Water Made Simple," *High Country News,* Paonia, Colo., (four special issues on Western water) Sept. 29, Oct. 13, Oct. 27, Nov. 10, 1986.

Reports and Studies

Driver, Bruce, "Western Water: Tuning the System," Western Governors' Association, July 7, 1986.

Editorial Research Reports: "Western Water: Coming Crisis," 1977 Vol. I, p. 21; "Western Land Policy," 1978 Vol. I, p. 81; "Rocky Mountain West: An Unfinished Country," 1980 Vol. I, p. 185.

El-Ashry, Mohamed T., and Diana C. Gibbons, "Troubled Waters: New Policies for Managing Water in the American West," October 1986, World Resources Institute.

Folk-Williams, John A., Susan C. Fry, and Lucy Hilgendorf, "Western Water Flows to the Cities," Western Network, 1985.

Meyer, Christopher, "Western Water Law in Transition: Showdown at the River," National Wildlife Federation Rocky Mountain Natural Resources Clinic, Boulder, Colo., 1986.

Postel, Sandra, "Water: Rethinking Management in an Age of Scarcity," December 1984; and "Conserving Water: The Untapped Alternative," September 1985, Worldwatch Institute, Washington, D.C.

Western States Water Council, "Indian Water Rights in the West," Western Governors' Association, May 1984.

Graphics: P. 125, California's Coachella Canal; photos pp. 129, 140, U.S. Bureau of Reclamation

DOLLAR

DIPLOMACY

by

Mary H. Cooper

**Mar. 13
1 9 8 7**

Editor's Note: The February agreement to stabilize the dollar's value proved less successful than anticipated. In mid-April, as the dollar resumed its slide, Treasury Secretary James A. Baker III took the unusual step of stating publicly that any further erosion of the dollar would be "counterproductive." By late April, the U.S. currency had fallen to a postwar low of 139.95 Japanese yen despite heavy intervention by the Federal Reserve and other central banks.

Baker's comment came 18 months after he had launched an international effort to reduce the dollar's value as a means of reversing the U.S. trade deficit. But even as the dollar's fall appeared to be slipping out of control, the trade balance had not improved, and protectionist sentiment grew in the United States. In mid-April, President Reagan imposed tariffs against some Japanese goods in retaliation for Japan's refusal to open its market to U.S. goods. Congress appeared ready to pass a trade bill that would require the president to retaliate against "unfair trading practices" by other countries.

Halting the Dollar's Fall

For the moment, at least, the Paris agreement by six of the world's major industrial powers to stabilize exchange rates seems to be working. Since the Feb. 22 meeting in Paris, the dollar has held steady against the Japanese yen and the West German mark, the world's other two most frequently traded currencies, indicating that foreign exchange markets have taken the pact seriously.

The agreement to halt the dollar's plunge came just two years after it reached a peak, at a time when the soaring greenback allowed Americans to see the world on the cheap and develop a taste for luxury imports. But what was good for American consumers was not beneficial for U.S. industry. In early 1985, as the dollar was at its peak, sales of imported cars rose 15 percent in this country, where dollars went further in the purchase of foreign goods because of the American currency's appreciation. But meanwhile, U.S. products languished on foreign markets, where it took more yen, marks and other currencies to buy American.

In early 1985, when Treasury Secretary James A. Baker III undertook the task of reversing the dollar's upward course, and America's trading fortunes, he faced stiff opposition. Even among allies, one country's strong currency is another's ticket to greater prosperity and not something to be given up without a struggle. Seen from Japan and West Germany, the strong dollar was a godsend, allowing their export industries to capture a bigger market share from American producers.

But America's hand was stronger by September of that year, after Baker resorted to currency intervention — in essence putting large amounts of dollars into circulation by trading them for other currencies through the Federal Reserve System. With the dollar falling, America's trading partners were mindful that their exports were becoming increasingly expensive. At a meeting at New York's Plaza Hotel, America, Britain, France, Japan and West Germany agreed for the first time to try to stabilize exchange rates, and world trade, by jointly intervening in their various currencies. *(See pp. 154-55.)*

Although the goal of stability had not been realized, the incentive for cooperation was even stronger when the nations met again at Paris this February. During the previous 12 months, the dollar had plunged faster and farther than America's trading partners intended, and Baker's case for a new joint agreement was far more persuasive.

After months of bickering, including independent efforts by Japan and Germany to strengthen their currencies, and the collapse of the Plaza accord, the stage was set for another agreement. In it, the five trading partners and Canada, which endorsed the pact negotiated by the others, agreed to resume joint management of exchange rates. At Baker's urging, they also went a step further, agreeing that America, West Germany and Japan would make domestic policy changes that would bring more balance among world trade accounts.

Pledges by Major Nations Are at Risk

The Paris agreement — which British finance minister Nigel Lawson dubbed "Plaza II" — was widely applauded as a difficult but necessary compromise. In theory, it is a significant step toward a jointly managed world economy. But in reality, its success is far from assured, particularly because of the policy promises that make the agreement unique. Pledges by Germany and Japan to stimulate consumer spending face stiff resistance at home because they are seen as running counter to the economic interests of those export-driven economies.

In the United States, the terms of the agreement may also face stiff opposition. America's promise, in effect to make $63 billion in reductions of the U.S. federal budget deficit over the next two years, will depend on the ability of President Reagan and a Democratic-controlled Congress to agree on a tax and spending plan that meets that goal. Though the reductions are mandated by the 1985 Balanced Budget Act (popularly known as Gramm-Rudman), wiping out that much budgetary red ink clearly will be no small task.

Meanwhile, the harm suffered by American industry when the dollar was strong continues to fuel calls for protective legislation. So far, the Reagan administration has been able to fend it off the main thrusts of protectionism, preferring instead to look for solutions in exchange rates and greater U.S. industrial "competitiveness." But if the exchange rate agreement does not bring relief, calls for protectionism almost certainly will intensify.

For American consumers, the weak dollar's impact has not yet been fully felt, as Japanese and European exporters of everything from bottled water to luxury automobiles have hesitated to pass along the higher price of their goods to the American buyer for fear of losing their foothold in a lucrative market. But the Paris agreement to hold exchange rates at about their present value could mean the era of bargain imports is coming to an end, forcing a change in American consumers' increasingly expensive taste for foreign imports. After all, the dollar's value had fallen about 50 percent against both the yen and the mark in the past two years.

Dollar Diplomacy

The Paris agreement is the latest in a series of attempts to stabilize world currency values since 1973, when the system of fixed exchange rates set up under the 1944 Bretton Woods Agreement was abandoned. Since 1973, the world's currencies have been allowed to "float," rising and falling in value according to supply and demand. As the movement of currencies across national boundaries has increased with expanding global trade and investment, exchange rates have become more volatile. For the United States, the impact has been especially great because the dollar is the principal currency of world trade.

The central component of the Paris accord is the agreement by the six trading partners that their currencies are now "within ranges broadly consistent with underlying economic fundamentals" and that they will act in concert to keep the dollar, mark and yen at about their present values. Although the parties were deliberately vague about how their agreement to "cooperate closely" will work, it presumably will entail intervention in currency markets by the U.S. Federal Reserve System and central banks in the other nations.

Trade Implications of a Devalued Dollar

An important implication of the agreement is that the trading partners will stop trying to use exchange rate variations as a means of forcing one another to change their positions on trade. In the weeks leading up to the Paris meeting, for example, it was said that Treasury Secretary Baker had "talked the dollar down" in an attempt to pressure West Germany and Japan to increase their imports of American products. By publicly denying charges that the dollar was falling too far, too fast, Baker had signaled that the United States was not about to remove massive quantities of dollars from circulation. The currency markets concluded from his remarks that there was no impending shortage of U.S. currency, and the dollar's value continued to plummet, thus threatening the export-driven West German and Japanese economies.

The Paris agreement made no explicit mention of specific ranges of acceptable currency fluctuations — known as "reference zones" — which Baker has long argued should be adopted. But in effect, the parties appear to have adopted the reference zone principle or something very similar. Under a reference zone agreement, finance ministers and central bankers of participating countries would be required to consult on measures to be taken whenever a currency's value passes beyond the established upper or lower limits of the zone. Whatever the precise terms of the Paris agreement, reference zones are likely to be the subject of discussion at the next annual economic summit meeting of heads of government in June.

While the long-awaited agreement on currency values levels is the central component of the Paris accord, it alone cannot be expected to resolve the trade problems created by volatile exchange rates. Central banks intervene in the foreign exchange market by either buying or selling large amounts of a currency to raise or lower its value against that of other currencies. But in recent years, as the volume of private funds related to foreign trade and investment has swelled on the foreign exchange market, the impact of government intervention on exchange rates has diminished. If central bank intervention is inadequate to stabilize exchange rates, then coordination of domestic economic policy — the other component of the Paris agreement — becomes all the more significant.

In that part of the Paris accord, Japan and West Germany both agreed to take steps which Baker had pushed for months but which both countries had resisted. While the United States posted a $170 billion trade deficit last year, Japan and West Germany enjoyed trade surpluses of $89 billion and $63 billion. By increasing their own consumer and business demand, the United States has argued, both trading partners could buy more American goods and services and bring the three countries' trade accounts into closer balance.

Germany and Japan: Two Approaches

From the American point of view, West Germany made the more striking policy reversal of the two trading partners. After vehemently resisting Baker's pleas for months, West Germany pledged to stimulate domestic growth by increasing the amount

---

How Intervention Works

Central banks can raise or lower the value of a country's currency, its "exchange rate" with other currencies, by buying or selling large amounts of it, thus making its supply more scarce or more plentiful. In America, the decision to intervene in the foreign exchange market is made jointly by the chairman of the Federal Reserve Board and the Treasury secretary. The Federal Reserve Board then orders the Federal Reserve Bank of New York, its operating arm, to carry out the transaction. The bank's trading desk buys or sells dollars through 100 major commercial bank dealers in New York, including some U.S. branches of foreign banks. If the goal is to make the dollar appreciate in value, the New York bank buys up large amounts of dollars, using other currencies. Conversely, it can sell dollars in exchange for other currencies in an effort to flood the market and bring down the dollar's exchange rate.

---

of tax cuts already planned for 1988 and by proceeding with a new tax reform measure that would give West German consumers more money to spend.

Japan's commitment to stimulate its economy with a "comprehensive" program was less specific and, to date, has resulted in no legislative proposal. Although the Bank of Japan cut its discount rate — the interest charged banks for short-term loans — by 0.5 percent to a postwar low of 2.5 percent the day before the Paris meeting, this move was not expected to have a significant impact on Japanese consumer demand because interest rates were already low. "[West] Germany has made a clear policy change in the right direction," said David D. Hale, chief economist of Kemper Financial Services in Chicago. "Japan is the real slowpoke."

In both West Germany and Japan, however, the pledges given at Paris face stiff political opposition. Both those economies were largely destroyed during World War II, and in the decades since both have emerged as major industrial powers on the basis of exports. For this reason, they are reluctant to adopt policies that would undercut their competitiveness on export markets. Current Japanese and West German budget policies are aimed not at consumer spending but at consumer saving, which provides investment capital for export industries.

Although the two countries reluctantly acceded to U.S. demands on exchange rates and fiscal policy, Japan and Germany continue to blame the United States for the trade and currency imbalances. By running huge federal budget deficits, they say, the United States created its own trade dilemma. By introducing policies to encourage savings rather than spending, they say, Washington could curtail the American consumer's appetite for imports without seeking budget policy concessions from its trading partners. Given these arguments, it will not be easy for the West German and Japanese governments to carry out the tax reform measures, spending cuts and interest rate reductions they promised in Paris.

Roles of U.S. Trade Partners

In Japan, the high yen — which has appreciated from 260 to about 150 yen to the dollar since early 1985 — has become a subject of widespread concern. American critics point to Japan's growing trade surplus with the United States, up from $19 billion in 1984 to $58.6 billion last year, the largest of any U.S.

trading partner. But the falling dollar has hurt Japan more than the other parties to the Paris agreement because it is the most dependent on exports to the American market, which account for nearly half of all Japan's foreign sales. Rising prices for Japanese exports, it is feared, could cause a recession. Although Japan's economy continued to grow last year, industrial production fell slightly for the first time since 1975 and unemployment rose to 6 percent, the highest level since the end of World War II. According to the Democratic Socialist Party, 705 Japanese companies have gone bankrupt in the two years since the yen began to appreciate against the dollar.

Amid concerns for the well-being of Japan's economy, Finance Minister Kiichi Miyazawa's Paris commitment to introduce "comprehensive" stimulative measures to the Japanese economy faces high political obstacles. The Japanese parliament, officially the Diet, has not even begun to discuss a tax reform and budget proposal, submitted shortly before the Paris meeting, that would have some stimulative effects. According to Masakazu Hayashi, counselor for financial affairs at the Japanese Embassy in Washington, the Nakasone government will not propose any additional stimulative measures until parliament votes on the budget and tax measure.

That proposal contains tax rate cuts. According to Hale, of Kemper Financial Services, it is an important step toward fiscal policy coordination by the two trading partners. If enacted, the proposal, together with the U.S. federal tax reform law that took effect in January, will bring about "fewer divergences in the microeconomic components of the two countries' fiscal systems than at any time since the Second World War." [1]

But the proposal's approval is far from certain. The opposition parties to Prime Minister Yasuhiro Nakasone's Liberal Democratic Party oppose it on the ground that a new sales tax, which is part of the proposal, would have a disproportionate impact on poorer citizens. Because the government is currently preoccupied with "making a great effort to persuade the opposition" to accept the sales tax, Hayashi said, "so far it has had no time to study new proposals for stimulating our economy."

Because the debate over the sales tax proposal could doom Nakasone's ambitions for re-election when his term expires in October, he may modify or retract the proposal, dimming prospects that Japan will enact any meaningful stimulative economic measures this year. Other measures advocated by critics

---

[1] David D. Hale, "Tax Reform in the U.S. and Japan: The Movement Towards International Tax Convergence," paper presented before the U.S.-Japan Consultative Group on International Monetary Affairs, San Diego, Calif., February 1987.

(continued on p. 156)

How U.S. Pressure on the Dollar . . .

Despite their position that the burden of correcting the low dollar rests on the United States, the Europeans and Japanese had little room to negotiate for better terms in Paris. As the dollar has fallen in the past year, their export industries have suffered, and fears of further damage to their trade positions prompted them to accept some of the U.S. demands.

An important factor in the dollar's fall has been a policy shift by the Reagan administration. In the president's first term, the United States adhered to a hands-off, free-market policy on exchange rates, proclaiming an end to the Carter administration's practice of intervening in currency markets to correct dollar fluctuations. The strong dollar, Reagan said early in his first term, was a sign that his policy of cutting taxes and government spending at home had restored international confidence in the American economy.

When the dollar soared against the mark and the yen in the early 1980s, pushed up in large part by high U.S. interest rates, the administration continued its policy of non-intervention until the rising flood of imports pushed the U.S. trade balance into deficit and forced a change of position. In January 1985, shortly before Treasury Secretary Donald T. Regan switched jobs with White House Chief of Staff James A. Baker III, Regan announced that the United States would intervene in the foreign exchange market to push down the dollar. In the wake of this policy reversal, the dollar began its decline after peaking in February 1985, when it traded for 263 yen and 3.44 marks.

Alarmed by the rising trade deficit, Baker sought greater coordination from America's trading partners to bring down the dollar's value. A September 1985 accord in New York, which was a vaguely worded agreement to coordinate exchange rate intervention between Baker and his counterparts from Britain, France, Japan and West Germany, convinced the foreign exchange markets that the trading partners would intervene heavily, pushing the dollar even faster on its downward path. However, the Plaza accord — named for the New York hotel where it was reached —fell apart in early 1986, as Japan and West Germany began to intervene, without success, to stem their own currencies' rapid appreciation.

Some U.S. officials, including Federal Reserve Board Chairman Paul A. Volcker, began to warn of the dangers presented by a "free fall" of the dollar. If the dollar declines too fast, he has said, foreign investors may panic and withdraw their money from U.S. investments, especially government securities, leaving the Treasury with insufficient funds to finance the federal budget deficit. Under such a worst-case scenario, the Fed would be forced either to create more money, fueling inflation, or raise interest rates in an effort to attract investors. Either course could prove devastating to the American economy.

Although the dollar's fall continued throughout 1986, it had no noticeable impact on the growing U.S. trade deficit. (Changes in

... Set the Stage for Paris Accord

currency values tend to have a delayed effect on trade patterns, in part because several years may pass between an initial order for a product, its manufacture and its delivery to the export market. Also, exporters often prefer to reduce their profits rather than risk losing market share.) As the trade deficit continued to grow, the Reagan administration found it increasingly hard to resist calls for protectionist legislation. Acknowledging the limited effectiveness of exchange rate intervention alone in correcting the trade deficit, Baker pressed Japan and West Germany to stimulate consumption. He was rebuffed by both countries, which expressed fear that such stimulative measures as tax cuts and lower interest rates would fuel inflation.

By the end of 1986, however, both West Germany and Japan were beginning to suffer the consequences of their currencies' appreciation against the dollar. Unemployment rose and economic growth slowed in both countries as their exporting industries were forced by the loss of profits to lay off workers and cut production. Efforts by the government of Japanese Prime Minister Yasuhiro Nakasone to depress the yen's value by exchange rate intervention proved fruitless, and the yen appreciated to a record of just under 150 to the dollar. Finance Minister Kiichi Miyazawa met with Baker in Washington in October and gave Japan's commitment to lower interest rates and introduce additional measures to stimulate the Japanese economy. It was also reported that the two sides agreed privately to adopt a "reference zone" — an idea most of the United States' other chief trading partners have so far rebuffed — and to take steps to hold the dollar's value within that zone of 150 to 163 yen.

The dollar's plunge accelerated this January, as it fell by 7.4 percent against the mark and 4.4 percent against the yen amid reports that Baker — disappointed by Japan's failure to stimulate its economy — was refraining from stemming the currency's fall to press Japan and West Germany to take further action. The same month, the seven nations belonging to the European Monetary System — Belgium, France, Italy, Ireland, Luxembourg, the Netherlands and West Germany — whose currencies are roughly pegged to the West German mark, were forced to realign their currencies under pressure from the mark's rise against the dollar. After the yen dipped below 150 against the dollar on Jan. 16, Miyazawa again traveled to Washington, but this time obtained no apparent commitment from Baker to stem the dollar's fall.

The Treasury secretary explained his tough stand on the dollar: "The United States has taken 60 percent of the increase in exports from lesser developed countries around the world. We'd like to see some of those exports going somewhere else as well and we'd like to see other industrialized countries that have big surpluses taking more exports from the United States." By mid-February the dollar had fallen still further against the yen and the mark, setting the stage for the Paris agreement combining exchange rate intervention with domestic policy changes.

(continued from p. 153)
of Japan's savings-oriented policy, such as easing restrictions on consumer loans and making financing for housing more accessible, seem unlikely to be considered in the foreseeable future.

Meanwhile, resentment grows in Japan over what is widely viewed as American highhandedness in Baker's "benign neglect" of the falling dollar. "If we continue like this, we will be slave laborers to the world forever," said one Japanese banker. "What Nakasone did was make one unilateral concession after another to President Reagan, always yielding to the U.S. demand that Japan be the one to initiate changes," another critic charged. "This is simply an extension of the attitude that has characterized Japanese relations with the U.S. since the close of the Pacific war." [2]

Inflation Fears Inhibit West Germany

West Germany, which is less dependent on the U.S. market for its exports than Japan, long resisted Baker's calls for a more stimulative domestic policy, refusing, for example, to join the United States and Japan in a currency stabilization agreement they made last October. West German officials cite fear of inflation as their main reason for refusing to go along with U.S. proposals, often recalling the last time West Germany bowed to American pleas to encourage consumption at home. After West Germany accepted President Carter's request that it serve as a "locomotive" to rescue the falling dollar in 1977-78, that country experienced inflation that was high by West German standards, though not as high as in the United States or the rest of Europe. One reason the fear of inflation is especially sharp in West Germany is the memory of post-World War I runaway inflation, which was the highest ever recorded anywhere.

Though reluctant to run the risk of an inflationary spiral, West Germany offered greater concessions in Paris in terms of domestic budget policy than Japan. On Feb. 25, just three days after the new pact, Gerhard Stoltenberg, the West German finance minister, went beyond his Paris commitment to increase the size of tax cuts scheduled for next year. He announced a $24 billion tax reform package to take effect between 1988 and 1990. The agreement resolved a dispute that had split the center-right governing coalition led by Chancellor Helmut Kohl since it was returned to power in elections held Jan. 25.

However, the tax cuts, which would cost about 19 billion marks ($10.3 billion), would be paid for in large part by reductions in West Germany's relatively high public expenditures.

---

[2] From the Japanese newspaper *Nihon Keizai Shimbun*, Jan. 17, 1987, cited in *World Press Review*, March 1987, p. 45.

"This will be hard to attain," a West German government official explained. "Each subsidy has its own political history that comes back to haunt you when you try to cut it." Faced with slowing economic growth caused in large part by the mark's increasing value against the dollar, he said, there are growing demands for subsidies. West German farmers, for example, are calling for higher subsidies to compensate for their cuts in agricultural production. And shipbuilders are asking for more government support to see them through the worldwide slump in that industry.

Adding to the political obstacles facing tax reform in West Germany are this year's elections, in four states, all of which depend to some degree on subsidies. In an effort to win the voters' support in these states, the German official said, "the government has announced the tax-cut goodies first and will not propose the subsidy cuts necessary to pay for them until after the elections," the last of which will be held in September.

The Kohl government, whose slim election victory is blamed on a recent weakening of the economy, is a reluctant party to the Paris agreement and remains ambivalent on its prospects for success. "The dollar is much too low now," the official said, "but we are realistic enough not to expect major rises in the near future." The German government is blunt in its negative assessment of the U.S. contribution to policy coordination, especially its failure to come to grips with the federal budget deficit. "The missing part of the agreement is a commitment by the Reagan administration to raise taxes," the German official said. Criticizing the administration's insistence that low taxes are vital to U.S. economic growth, the official added, "Europeans in their simple-mindedness see things differently, that taxes must be raised to cut the budget deficit."

Until recently, the Kohl government rebuffed American calls to stimulate the West German economy, saying it was already growing fast enough. The falling dollar, however, pushed West Germany into the agreement with its trading partners. As the dollar has plummeted from its 1985 peak of 3.46 marks to about 1.80 today, West German exporters have faced the same dilemma as the Japanese: either lose markets to competitors with weaker currencies or absorb the cost of the high mark by trimming profits and cutting production. West German Unemployment, already high by U.S. standards, shot up from 8.9 percent in December to 10 percent in January. Despite a record trade surplus last year, growth in exports, which account for 30 percent of the West German economy, was a disappointing 0.06 percent, and many observers predict the beginning of a recession by this summer.

157

Comparing Exchange Rates

Index 1980 = 100

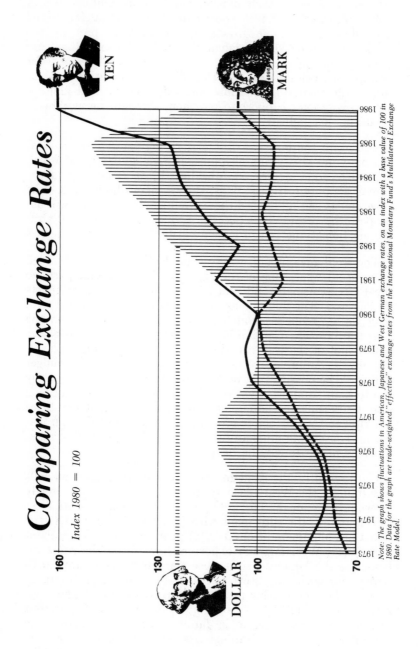

YEN

MARK

DOLLAR

160

130

100

70

1973 1974 1975 1976 1977 1978 1979 1980 1981 1982 1983 1984 1985 1986

Note: The graph shows fluctuations in American, Japanese and West German exchange rates, on an index with a base value of 100 in 1980. Data for the graph are trade-weighted "effective" exchange rates from the International Monetary Fund's Multilateral Exchange Rate Model.

How Britain, France, Canada are Faring

West Germany's faltering performance is of special concern to Britain and France, the other European parties to the Paris agreement, because West Germany is the region's leading economic power, fueling growth among its neighbors. Further linking France's economic health to that of West Germany, the franc is loosely pegged to the mark through the European Monetary System (EMS). As the mark has appreciated against the dollar, so has the French currency, reducing the competitiveness of French exports. The falling dollar's effects began to be felt toward the end of last year. French unemployment rose above 10 percent at the end of 1986, as industrial production fell in the last quarter of the year. Italy's lira also is pegged to the mark through the EMS. But in contrast to France, Italy has continued to grow at a healthy pace, leading many analysts to predict that it may overtake Britain this year in total output.

The British pound sterling, which has been superseded by the mark as Western Europe's dominant currency, has been kept independent of the EMS by Prime Minister Margaret Thatcher's Conservative government in the belief that the pound would maintain a better value outside the system. The pound has in fact weakened as the other European currencies have risen, giving British industry a needed shot in the arm. As a result, British exports to West Germany, other European countries and Japan have increased, contributing to Britain's falling unemployment and rising productivity and profits. The dollar has fallen by 12 percent against the pound over the past year, less than it has relative to other currencies.

Canada, which is America's biggest trading partner and the sixth party to the Paris agreement, has seen its currency firm only slightly against the dollar. Thus its trade position has been relatively unchanged. Though Canada endorsed the pact, it was not in on the negotiations.

In a note of discord in Paris, Italy refused to endorse the agreement, saying its and Canada's exclusion from the negotiations violated an understanding reached last May that any discussion of exchange rate management would include all of the so-called Group of Seven nations, which have been coordinating economic policy since 1975.

U.S. Deficit-Cutting Pledge

In the United States, the weak dollar has yet to benefit U.S. export industries significantly. "There are straws in the wind," said Lawrence A. Fox, vice president in charge of international economic affairs for the National Association of Manufacturers. Signs of improvement attributable to the falling dollar are beginning to appear among chemicals and some other basic commodities as well as in European orders for U.S. producer goods, he said. "But last year exports grew by just 2 percent, while imports grew by 7 percent, so we are not yet back to 1981 trade levels."

Although the United States is less dependent than its major trading partners on exports, they are increasingly important for the country's economic health. In addition, industries that are not heavily export-dependent are being displaced from the domestic market by more efficient foreign competitors. Calls for government protection are thus likely to mount, despite the Reagan administration's warning that protectionist legislation would set off a trade war between the United States and its trading partners.

To many European observers, the coming budget negotiations between the President and Congress loom as a major obstacle to the Paris agreement. "It is impossible to tie Congress by an agreement with five or six ministers of finance," the West

Treasury Secretary James A. Baker III

German official observed. In contrast, he added, European governments have much more leverage over their parliaments. In Britain and West Germany, for example, the prime minister or chancellor is named by the majority in parliament, which thus has a moral obligation to support the government. "European leaders confer with parliament before meetings like the one in Paris and thus they go to them with their parliaments' firm support; the United States has no such guarantee," the official concluded.

Indeed, Treasury Secretary Baker faces an uphill battle with Congress over his pledge that America will meet the budget targets that were mandated by the 1985 Balanced Budget Act. Many observers say both tax increases and spending cuts are needed to meet the $108 billion deficit target for fiscal 1988. In Congress, House Speaker Jim Wright, D-Texas, has come out in support of a tax hike. But the administration continues to reject the idea. In the absence of a tax increase, the Congressional Budget Office estimates that government spending will have to be cut by $63 billion if the target is to be met, a goal few congressional observers say is feasible.

Pessimism that Budget Cuts Will Be Big

As they confronted the task of drafting the fiscal 1988 budget resolution in late February, the House and Senate Budget Committee chairmen, Rep. William H. Gray III, D-Pa., and Sen. Lawton Chiles, D-Fla., said they expected to obtain no more than a $36 billion-$40 billion cut. Further diminishing chances the deficit target will be met is the prospect of the 1988 presidential election. With an eye on that race, members of both parties in Congress likely will be reluctant to support spending cuts or tax increases.

Nevertheless, Federal Reserve Board chairman Paul A. Volcker continues to caution that deficit reduction cannot be put off much longer. Although he concedes that the $108 billion target figure may be unrealistic, he has warned that any reduction in the trade deficit brought on by the dollar's fall will not benefit the American economy unless the budget deficit is reduced at the same time and by roughly the same amount. Because a shrinking trade deficit would be accompanied by a reduction in the volume of foreign capital flowing into the United States, the Fed chairman warns, the government's borrowing must also shrink to avoid competing too strongly with private business for a smaller supply of lendable funds. "The clear implication would be congested capital markets, higher interest rates, strong inflationary dangers, and threats to growth," Volcker concluded in testimony before the Senate Budget Committee on Feb. 25.

Korea and Taiwan: Fortunate Exceptions

While most of the major strong-currency countries have been feeling the pinch as the dollar has depreciated over the past year, for Taiwan and South Korea the plunge has been beneficial. Because their currencies have fallen along with the dollar, the exports of these newly industrialized trading nations have become increasingly competitive against those of Japan and some West European nations.

Exporters on the island of Taiwan have gained a strong foothold in Japan and Western Europe as a result of the falling dollar, to which Taiwan's dollar is loosely pegged. Taiwan's trade surplus with the United States, to which Taiwan ships half its exports, reached a record $13.6 billion in 1986. The trade imbalance has brought Taiwan under heavy fire by U.S. critics of its stiff tariffs, which block U.S. and other imports.

Although Taiwan is now counted among the nine major industrial powers and enjoyed the third-largest trade surplus with the United States after Japan and Canada last year, Taiwan still receives trade preferences the United States grants developing countries to help their export industries. Under pressure from Washington, the Taiwanese government has intervened in the local foreign exchange market, causing an 11 percent appreciation of the Taiwan dollar against the U.S. dollar last year.

Although South Korea's currency, the won, is not officially pegged to the dollar, it has fallen in tandem with the U.S. currency as a result of successive devaluations aimed at enhancing the country's export industries. Unlike Taiwan, however, South Korea has resisted U.S. pressure to raise the won's value. Exports to Japan and Western Europe allowed South Korea to register its first trade surplus in years in 1986, bringing in capital it needs to reduce its $45 billion national debt.

The good fortune of Taiwan and South Korea did not escape the notice of the parties to the Paris exchange rate agreement. In their closing statement they added their voice to the pressure on the newly industrialized nation to assume some of the burdens of industrial development and expanding trade. The statement urged the newly industrialized countries to "allow their currencies to reflect more fully underlying economic fundamentals."

Meanwhile, administration hopes of deflecting calls for protectionist legislation appear increasingly dim. Last year was the fifth in a row in which Americans bought more goods and services from other countries than they sold overseas. Recent statistics indicate that another record trade deficit may be set in 1987. The administration, which last year vetoed a bill passed by Congress that would have curbed textile imports and some other commodities, this year has introduced its own trade bill in an attempt to fend off Democratic-sponsored proposals calling for import restrictions.[3] In another move aimed at derailing protectionism, the administration has launched a campaign aimed at improving U.S. industrial competitiveness.

---

[3] The Reagan administration's trade proposal was introduced Feb. 19 in both the House (HR 1155) and Senate (S 539). Cosponsors are Senate Minority Leader Robert Dole, R-Kan., and House Minority Leader Robert H. Michel, R-Ill.

Recommended Reading List

Books

Kaufman, Henry. *Interest Rates, the Markets, and the New Financial World*, Times Books, 1986.

Strange, Susan, *Casino Capitalism*, Basil Blackwell, 1986.

Articles

Brownstein, Vivian, "Fortune Forecast: Where the Dollar Is Headed — With Luck," *Fortune,* Feb. 16, 1987.

Dryden, Steven J., "The Risks of a Free-Fall," *Business Week,* Feb. 2, 1987.

Durant, Andrew, and Ira Kaminow, "The Dollar and the Search for Stability: What Are the Implications for Japan?" *The JAMA Forum* (published by the Japan Automobile Manufacturers Association Inc.), Jan. 10, 1987.

Fallows, James, "The Rice Plot," *The Atlantic,* January 1987.

Hale, David D., "The United States in Opposition, or, Can Mr. Baker Prevent Germany and Japan From Pushing the World Back into Recession," *Japan Economic Journal,* January 1987.

Reports and Studies

Ito, Takatoshi, "The Intra-Daily Exchange Rate Dynamics and Monetary Policies After the G5 Agreement," National Bureau of Economic Research, October 1986.

EUROMISSILE

NEGOTIATIONS

by

Mary H. Cooper

Apr. 24
1 9 8 7

Removing Europe's Warheads

The fate of the most promising superpower arms control negotiations in years may depend as much on London, Paris and Bonn as on Washington and Moscow. The three-day talks in Moscow between Secretary of State George P. Shultz and Foreign Minister Eduard A. Shevardnadze and Shultz' meeting with Soviet leader Mikhail S. Gorbachev ended April 15 with optimistic predictions on both sides of an early agreement on the removal of medium-range nuclear missiles from Europe. Tass, the official Soviet news agency, called the talks "timely and useful," while Shultz said that "very considerable headway" had been made, adding that "it should be possible to work out an agreement."

But the secretary of state stressed that acceptance of a new Soviet proposal to eliminate short-range nuclear missiles would depend on the consent of America's West European allies. "We are a member of a strong alliance and on matters of this importance, of course, we don't respond immediately," he said. "We consult carefully with our allies." Shultz went directly to Brussels to discuss the proposal with America's increasingly skittish European allies, who are concerned that a reduction in U.S. nuclear weapons in Europe would leave their countries vulnerable to Soviet conventional forces and weaken nuclear deterrence.

Indeed, the vision of a nuclear-free world is sending shock waves through the continent. Fearful that the United States may decouple its strategic interests from those of Europe, British Prime Minister Margaret Thatcher dismissed that vision as "a dream" when she visited Moscow several weeks ago. "You cannot base a sure defense on dreams," she told Gorbachev, who has proposed that all nuclear weapons be eliminated within the next 10-15 years.

President Reagan, who initially welcomed Gorbachev's proposal during their October 1986 summit meeting in Reykjavik, Iceland, has since backed away from the idea. But the leaders of America's strongest European allies aren't leaving it to America to press their case. Although the official parties to these negotiations are the United States and the Soviet Union, Western Europe is emerging as a highly visible third party intent upon impressing its interests on any agreement between the superpowers. In taking Western Europe's case to Moscow, Thatcher signaled a widespread concern that the Reagan administration — eager to put behind it the debilitating scandal over the secret Iran-contra arms deal — will rush into an arms agreement that fundamentally alters traditional military strategy in Europe.

The European allies are playing a greater part in these East-West talks than they did during negotiations that led to the SALT (Strategic Arms Limitation Talks) agreements limiting long-range nuclear weapons, test ban treaties and other nuclear arms pacts. These were made between Moscow and Washington largely over the heads of their allies.

Thatcher Presses for Third-Party Voice

Thatcher has become Europe's chief broker in the U.S.-Soviet negotiations over the removal of Soviet and U.S. medium- and short-range nuclear missiles, known as "Euromissiles," that are deployed in or within range of Europe. Britain and France are the only members of the 16-nation North Atlantic Treaty Organization (NATO) besides the United States that possess their own nuclear weapons, while West Germany, as NATO's front-line state, hosts the greatest number of U.S. medium-range nuclear weapons aimed at the Soviet Union and its Eastern European allies of the Warsaw Pact.[1] Before her highly publicized trip to Moscow, Thatcher conferred with France's President François Mitterrand and West Germany's Chancellor Helmut Kohl. In Moscow, she presented Gorbachev with their consensus that any Euromissile agreement should include NATO's right to deploy short-range nuclear missiles, a class of weapons currently deployed by the Warsaw Pact alone.

In retrospect, Thatcher's message to Gorbachev may have heralded the touchiest aspect of the negotiations on the Euromissiles, which were set to resume on April 23 in Geneva. When Gorbachev announced the surprise Soviet offer to remove the short-range missiles, it was widely viewed as so attractive the United States would have to say yes. But as Thatcher made plain to Gorbachev, Europe has misgivings. Even if NATO ultimately endorses a Euromissile deal, the current divergence between Europe and America may bring to the surface other differing interests within the alliance.

The United States will face the budgetary issue of who will pay the NATO bill for the increased cost of strengthening Western Europe's conventional defenses if the nuclear missiles are removed. As a cost-conscious Congress searches for ways to reduce the federal budget deficit and chafes under the country's growing trade deficit with Western Europe, it can be expected to press its allies to pay their own way in conventional defense.

Western European countries may be less reluctant than in the past to increase defense spending if the missiles are removed. They have already taken steps to coordinate conventional arms

---

[1] The Soviet Union's allies in Eastern Europe, signers of the Treaty of Warsaw in 1955, are Bulgaria, Czechoslovakia, East Germany, Hungary, Poland and Romania.

production, and there is talk of closer defense policy consultation among the 14 European members of the alliance — all except the United States and Canada. While this may be welcomed by congressional budget-cutters, it poses a threat to trans-Atlantic cohesion. A splintered alliance would give Gorbachev far more than a missile agreement.

America's Nuclear Umbrella over Europe

Since its creation as a defensive alliance in 1949, NATO has based its strategy on maintaining a combination of conventional and nuclear forces. While the U.S. nuclear umbrella has been the foundation of NATO's deterrent from the beginning, since 1967 the alliance has relied to a greater degree than previously on conventional forces. This "flexible response" strategy is to deter an attack by making the Soviet Union unsure whether NATO would respond with a limited conventional defense or all-out nuclear retaliation.

The medium-range missiles that are the main object of the current negotiations are relatively recent ingredients in the nuclear arsenals of both sides. The Soviets began deploying their SS-20 missile in 1977 as a longer-range, more accurate alternative to older, fixed-based SS-4 and SS-5 missiles. The SS-20 is mounted on a mobile launcher, so that it is less vulnerable than its fixed-based predecessors. It is armed with three warheads that can be aimed at separate targets up to 3,100 miles away. Thus the 441 SS-20s deployed in the European region of the Soviet Union — west of the Ural Mountains — and in the Soviet Far East, where the mobile missiles could easily be transported within range of Europe, carry a total of 1,323 nuclear warheads. In addition, 112 single-warhead SS-4s are still deployed in the western Soviet Union, within range of Europe.

The United States began developing the medium-range Pershing II and ground-launched cruise missiles as early as 1972. But the impetus for their deployment in Western Europe came initially from America's European allies in response to the Soviets' SS-20 deployment. The Europeans were concerned that the rough parity in U.S. and Soviet strategic nuclear forces that was codified in SALT I in 1972 and refined in talks leading up to the unratified SALT II agreement left the allies exposed to an imbalance in battlefield nuclear weapons and conventional forces in Europe. In 1977, then-West German Chancellor Helmut Schmidt warned that the SALT process would inevitably impair Western Europe's security if disparities in Soviet and European military power were not removed.

In 1979, NATO announced that it would begin deploying 108 Pershing II and 464 cruise missiles in Europe beginning in late

1983 unless a negotiated withdrawal of the Soviet SS-20s and SS-4s was obtained before that time. To date, 316 single-warhead missiles — 108 Pershing IIs and 208 cruise missiles — have been placed there.

The Pershings are all based in West Germany, where they replaced a similar number of shorter-range Pershing IA nuclear missiles. Although its range of about 1,100 miles is shorter than that of opposing Soviet missiles, the Pershing II can reach the Soviet Union from European positions. Its handicap of a single warhead is overcome by far-greater accuracy than the SS-20 achieves.[2]

The ground-launched cruise missiles have a range of 1,600 miles, longer than the Pershing's. For that reason, and because West Germany insisted that it not be the only NATO nation to deploy Euromissiles, cruise missiles have been based farther from the Eastern European border, in Belgium, Britain and Italy, as well as West Germany. If the negotiations fail to produce agreement removing medium-range missiles from Europe, 256 more cruise missiles are due to be installed in Britain, West Germany, Belgium and the Netherlands by the end of 1988.

Negotiating Twists and Turns Since 1980

Negotiations between the United States and the Soviet Union over reducing medium-range nuclear weapons in Europe began in 1980 in Geneva. But until the Iceland summit, the talks were essentially deadlocked over how many missiles should be allowed on both sides and where they should be deployed.

The United States sought equal global limits on U.S. and Soviet medium-range missiles, no matter where they are based. The ceiling would apply to Pershing IIs and ground-launched cruise missiles in Europe, but not to the separate nuclear forces of Britain and France. These, the American negotiators argued, are not under U.S. control. On the Soviet side, the United States wanted the ceiling to apply to all SS-20 and SS-4 missiles, including those in the Soviet Far East and on the eastern slopes of the Urals, which could be moved to positions that would threaten NATO. The American position also included a temporary freeze at equal levels on short-range missiles, whose fate would be determined later along with that of medium-range aircraft capable of carrying nuclear warheads.

The Soviet Union wanted to set equal limits on European-based missiles, but wanted to exclude missiles based elsewhere. The limits thus would not apply to the mobile SS-20s outside

---

[2] See Raymond L. Garthoff, *Détente and Confrontation* (1985), p. 799.

Europe. In addition, the Soviets wanted the agreement to apply to the nuclear forces of Britain and France.

So far, the Geneva negotiations have failed to reconcile these opposing positions. They were suspended for 16 months when the Soviet delegation walked out in November 1983, protesting the deployment of the Pershing II and cruise missiles that had just begun. But in January 1986, Soviet negotiatiors made the first of several major concessions. They changed their position on medium-range missiles in Asia, putting these forces on the negotiating table for the first time and offering to freeze their number.

At the Iceland summit, when Reagan and Gorbachev moved closer to breaking the Euromissile deadlock. They agreed to eliminate all medium-range missiles from Europe except those of the British and French forces. However, the agreement fell apart over the strategic defense initiative, when Reagan refused to meet the Soviet demand that the United States give up testing the planned U.S. space-based ballistic missile defense.

Gorbachev's offer on Feb. 28 of this year to separate the Euromissile negotiations from talks on long-range strategic nuclear weapons and from the strategic defense initiative lifted another major obstacle. At the same time, he made his "zero option" offer to remove from Europe all U.S. and Soviet nuclear missiles with ranges of 600-3,000 miles. The proposal — actually a reformulation of one advanced by Reagan in 1981 — called for the removal over five years of all Soviet SS-20 and SS-4 missiles and all U.S. Pershing II and ground-launched cruise missiles from Europe.

Under the agreement, each superpower would be allowed to keep 100 medium-range warheads in home territory outside Europe, though their deployment sites remain uncertain. The Soviet Union has proposed basing its 100 missiles on the eastern slopes of the Ural Mountains, while the United States has insisted they be stationed 1,000 miles farther east, well out of range of Europe. The U.S. suggestion to base its 100 missiles in Alaska, just across the Bering Strait from Siberia, is unlikely to be accepted by Soviet negotiators.

Because the Soviet Union currently has 1,435 warheads, and the United States only 316, an agreement to eliminate all but 100 on each side would appear to benefit NATO at Soviet expense. Indeed, when Reagan first proposed the zero option, the Soviets rejected it out of hand. Many observers say that the Reagan administration knew the Soviets would dismiss the proposal and made it only to counter criticism that it was uninterested in arms control.

GREENLAND
(Denmark)

ICELAND

NORWAY

North Sea

Baltic Sea

DENMARK
NETH.

SOVIET UNION

BRITAIN

Atlantic Ocean

BEL. LUX.
E. GER.
POLAND
W. GER.
CZECH.
HUNG.
ROMANIA

FRANCE

ITALY

BULG.

Black Sea

PORTUGAL
SPAIN

GREECE

TURKEY

Mediterranean Sea

NATO countries

Warsaw Pact Countries

Conventional Weapons

	NATO	WARSAW PACT
Combat aircraft and attack helicopters	3,700	8,000
Troop divisions	90	133
Battle tanks	19,600	32,000
Antitank weapons launchers	13,370	18,000

Source: Defense Department

Euromissiles

Medium-range

	Launchers	Warheads
U.S./NATO		
Pershing II	108	108
Ground-launched cruise missiles	52	208
		316
USSR/Warsaw Pact		
SS-20	441	1323
SS-4	112	112
		1435

Short-range

U.S./NATO	0	0
USSR/Warsaw Pact		
SS-23	20+	20+
SS-12/22	110	110
		130+

Note: Data includes 171 Soviet SS-20s based in Soviet Asia and 80+ short range missiles kept in the Soviet Union. NATO plans to deploy an additional 256 ground-launched cruise missiles by the end of 1988.

Source: Arms Control Association.

But whatever reservations the administration might have over the zero option, it was hard to refuse when Gorbachev dropped his demand that America give up testing of its planned space-based anti-ballistic missile defense. Four days later, U.S. negotiators presented a counterproposal at Geneva, and expressed confidence that an agreement could be reached in time for a treaty-signing summit between Reagan and Gorbachev in the United States before the end of the year. When Shultz traveled to Moscow and the Soviets unveiled their offer to remove their short-range missiles, the deal became more interesting from America's standpoint. However, the reaction in Western Europe was decidedly cooler toward the proposed pact.

Fear of 'Nuclear Nakedness'

G orbachev's offer to open new talks on short-range missiles in Europe on the eve of Shultz' arrival in Moscow was clearly made for Western European consumption. Fears among the European NATO allies that a reduction in nuclear forces would leave them vulnerable to attack by Warsaw Pact conventional forces and the friction those fears have created within the Western alliance constitute powerful leverage for Moscow because of the potential for divisiveness within NATO. The offer served to put Europe on notice that lack of progress in Moscow would not be for any lack of Soviet good will.

The Soviet leader's call upon "Paris, London and Bonn also to contribute" to the arms control process underscored Moscow's awareness of the trans-Atlantic debate over the consequences of a Euromissile agreement. In acknowledging that "there naturally is an asymmetry in the armed forces of the two sides in Europe" and offering to reduce "the numbers on the side which has a superiority in them," Gorbachev played to Western Europe's concern over the Warsaw Pact's numerical superiority in conventional forces.

Soviet Superiority in Conventional Arms

Until recent years, the disparity was offset by NATO's better weaponry, as well as its nuclear deterrent. But technological advances in Soviet weaponry and the Eastern alliance's advantage in troop strength have shifted the balance. According to U.S. Defense Department figures, the Warsaw Pact has 133 divisions in Europe or capable of being deployed there rapidly, against NATO's combined troop strength of 90 divisions. The Soviet Union and its allies field 32,000 battle tanks, compared with NATO's 19,600. NATO has only 13,370 anti-tank guided weapon launchers to combat this larger number of tanks, while the Warsaw Pact has 18,000. In the air, too, the Warsaw Pact holds a more than 2-to-1 advantage, with 8,000 combat aircraft and attack helicopters compared with NATO's 3,700.

Conventional weapons would become more significant to Europe's defense if short-range nuclear weapons were out of the picture. That is why Europe looks askance at the Soviet offer to remove its 130 short-range missiles. America's European allies had strongly supported the earlier U.S. position that would have equalized short-range missiles by allowing NATO to build up its force to a level equal with the Soviet force. That position was reiterated by Thatcher in Moscow. "We would like the right to match" the number of Soviet short-range weapons, she said, adding that the issue "might hold up complete agreement" on medium-range missiles. Labeling Gorbachev's goal of a nuclear-free world a "dream," she said, "Conventional weapons have never been enough to deter a war."

For weeks prior to Shultz' visit to Moscow, Soviet rejection of this demand was the main stumbling block to an agreement. Then Gorbachev's surprise offer to remove the Soviet short-range missiles, which have ranges from 300-600 miles, presented a new possibility for equalizing the short-range forces. But it wasn't the option many Europeans would have preferred.

The United States has no missiles in this category. The Soviet Union has about 110 launchers for its 540-mile-range SS-12/22s based in Eastern Europe and the western Soviet Union. More than 20 launchers for the 300-mile-range SS-23s are also based in the western Soviet Union.

Nuclear Weaponry that Would Remain

Of course, the actual balance of military power that would exist under Gorbachev's proposal is not so heavily skewed toward the Soviet bloc as might appear at first glance. Even under the most sweeping Euromissile proposal, eliminating both medium- and short-range missiles, Europe would not be free of nuclear weapons or denuded of the deterrent value they represent. In addition to the independent nuclear forces of Britain and France, there are 400 U.S. submarine-launched missiles available to NATO, and 116 U.S. F-111 bombers based in Britain for NATO. These aircraft can be armed with as many as three nuclear gravity bombs each and have a greater range than the Pershing missiles.

Also, Western Europe has hundreds of battlefield nuclear weapons, with ranges of less than 300 miles, which would not be limited by current the Euromissile proposal. In all, there are about 207 such missiles in Western Europe. Some 108 U.S. Lance missiles with a range of 66 miles are based in West Germany, and an additional 55 are controlled by West Germany, Italy, Belgium, the Netherlands and Britain. When Shultz met with Western European officials in Brussels, he emphasized that battlefield nuclear weapons were "not on the table" and "not part of these negotiations."

According to outgoing Assistant Secretary of Defense Richard N. Perle, there are now 4,600 U.S. nuclear weapons in Europe, and that number could be maintained following removal of medium- and short-range missiles by redeploying to Europe warheads not covered under the agreement. "And that," he said, "is hardly leaving our allies naked in front of the Soviet Union." [3]

Paul H. Nitze, President Reagan's adviser on arms control, has said of the 400 submarine-launched nuclear ballistic missile warheads available to NATO: "Given these remaining systems, as well as our extensive conventional contribution to NATO's defense," talk of decoupling Europe's strategic interests from America's is "unjustified." [4] Finally, the United States is committed under the 1949 North Atlantic Treaty to the notion that "an armed attack" against any NATO ally "shall be considered an attack against them all" and therefore to calling into play its U.S.-based strategic ballistic missiles, if necessary, to defend its allies.

European Doubts about America's Resolve

But Europeans ask whether Washington would risk Chicago to save Bonn. Many suspect it would not. And they point to repeated instances of ambivalent U.S. statements and actions to justify their less than total faith in America's nuclear umbrella.

For example, the Nixon administration's pronouncements in 1973 on the possibility of a limited nuclear war were seen by many Europeans as an alarming deviation from the postwar strategy of "mutual assured destruction." According to that strategy, any nuclear attack by either superpower would result in the annihilation of both. President Carter's support in 1977 for the idea of testing a neutron bomb produced a similar outcry. Especially in West Germany, where the enhanced radiation weapon would presumably have been deployed, popular condemnation of this "bomb to kill people but not buildings" was strong enough eventually to scuttle the project. When the Senate in 1979 balked at ratifying the nuclear arms limits of the SALT II agreement, Europe's hopes of easing East-West ten-

---

[3] Perle was interviewed April 17 in a CBS News television broadcast.
[4] Writing in *The Washington Post,* March 30, 1987.

sions and slowing the arms race received a blow, creating new suspicions about U.S. nuclear policy.

These suspicions have grown during the Reagan administration, which has been openly critical of the arms control process. France, Belgium, Sweden and the Netherlands deplored Reagan's decision last November to break out of the arms ceilings set by SALT II.[5] Although the treaty remained unratified, both sides observed its limits. Even such staunchly conservative Reagan supporters as Thatcher and Kohl have expressed doubts about the strategic defense initiative and criticized the administration's attempt to reinterpret the 1972 Antiballistic Missile (ABM) Treaty so as to allow the United States to proceed with testing components of the space-based missile defense system. According to the traditional interpretation of the treaty, which limits ABM weapons, testing of space-based weapons is prohibited.

But it was the stated agreement between Reagan and Gorbachev during their Iceland summit on the desirability of a nuclear-free world that has most alarmed America's Western European allies. Aghast at the prospect that Reagan would suddenly scrap the nuclear deterrent, Thatcher, speaking for the British, French and West German governments, rushed to Reagan's official retreat at Camp David, Md., where she obtained Reagan's agreement to seek limits on nuclear weapons rather than their elimination. Since that meeting last November, administration officials have backed away from the proposal to eliminate all nuclear weapons, conditioning this long-term goal on achieving parity in conventional forces, greater openness in Soviet society and a treaty on chemical weapons.

While a Euromissile agreement would not remove all nuclear weapons from Europe, America's NATO allies worry that it could be viewed by the Soviet Union and its allies as a decoupling of U.S. security interests from those of the Western Europeans. "They would be vulnerable, they could be preempted, they could be saturated," said Christoph Bertram, a West German military analyst. "Then you could think of limiting nuclear conflict to Europe. This is one of the nightmares of the Europeans: conflict in general, but [especially] *nuclear* conflict limited specifically to Europe."[6]

In America, former Secretary of State Henry A. Kissinger shares the European skepticism about the zero option. Although the Soviet Union would be forced to give up a greater number of

---

[5] On Nov. 28, 1986, the United States exceeded the 1,320 limit on nuclear warhead delivery systems when the Air Force deployed a B-52 bomber capable of carrying cruise missiles.

[6] Bertram was interviewed in *Arms Control Today*, January/February 1987, p.17.

warheads than the United States under the zero option, he writes, "what they give up in warheads they gain in political, psychological and diplomatic dissociation between the United States and Europe." [7] Kissinger has proposed making removal of the last Pershing II and cruise missiles conditional upon an agreement to achieve parity in short-range nuclear and conventional forces. John Deutch, Brent Scowcroft and R. James Woolsey, former Carter administration officials who are also critical of the zero option, favor leaving the 100 missiles allowed under the current proposal in Europe instead of withdrawing them to U.S. territory.

Verification Debate over Tactical Weapons

Another aspect of a Euromissile pact that is highly controversial in Europe is verification. The Soviet Union has long resisted U.S. attempts to include on-site inspection of weapons installations and production facilities as part of bilateral arms control agreements. Verification has been limited to information received via satellite and other information-gathering facilities outside the territories under surveillance. But this time it may be the Western alliance that will drag its feet on verification. It remains to be seen whether all five NATO allies involved in the Euromissile agreement — Belgium, Britain, Italy, the Netherlands and West Germany — will go along with the idea of Soviet military personnel inspecting their facilities.

The verification issue will be even murkier if limits on short-range missiles are included in the agreement. Most of these weapons are even smaller and more mobile than the Soviet SS-20s, so that on-site inspection of their deployment sites and production facilities would be even more critical. Some of these weapons, the SS-21 and SS-23 missiles, are also used as conventional weapons by arming them with nonnuclear warheads. Any ban on their use as nuclear weapons would complicate verification arrangements because it would be a simple matter to replace their conventional warheads with nuclear ones unless NATO inspectors were allowed frequent and sudden access to Warsaw Pact military installations.

The Euromissile talks have added a new and ironic twist to the verification issue. Whereas critics of arms control in the United States have long cited Soviet resistance to on-site verification to bolster their claims of Soviet non-compliance with existing treaties, there are signs that NATO may pose an obstacle to agreement on verification of a Euromissile pact. The United States would like to see highly intrusive inspection rights included in any agreement. Because the Pershing IIs and

---

[7] Writing in *The Washington Post*, April 5, 1987.

cruise missiles, as well as shorter-range weapons that may also be covered by an agreement, are produced in the United States, this would entail Soviet inspection of privately owned munitions factories as well as government-controlled storage areas.

The Soviets appear more willing to accept this arrangement than in the past. But in addition to a permanent Soviet presence in the United States, and an American presence in the

---

Speaking of Missiles

BALLISTIC MISSILES Rocket-launched missiles that approach their targets as free-falling projectiles after the rocket thrust is terminated. Long-range ballistic missiles travel outside the Earth's atmosphere in the middle portion of their trajectory. The U.S. Pershing IIs and the Soviet SS-20s and SS-4s that are being discussed in the Euromissile negotiations are medium-range ballistic missiles. In contrast, U.S. ground-launched cruise missiles are self-propelled guided missiles that fly inside the earth's atmosphere on the way to their targets.

EUROMISSILES A catchall term describing the medium- and short-range nuclear missiles based within range of Eastern and Western Europe over the past decade. In the current U.S.-Soviet negotiations, Euromissiles include medium and short-range missiles based in Europe and in both the Asian and European parts of the Soviet Union. The Soviet missiles are in range of Europe or could quickly be moved within range. Until 1981, Euromissiles were known officially as "theater nuclear forces." Now they are officially designated as intermediate-range nuclear forces.

INTERMEDIATE-RANGE NUCLEAR FORCES (INF) The medium-range nuclear missiles in the current Euromissile negotiations — the U.S. Pershing II and ground-launched cruise missiles and the Soviet SS-20s and SS-4s — are referred to in ongoing Geneva arms control negotiations between the superpowers as long-range INF missiles (LRINFs). These have ranges of about 1,500-3,000 miles. So-called short-range INF missiles (SRINFs) — which include the Soviet SS-12/22 and SS-23 missiles that are part of the Euromissile negotiations — have ranges of about 300-600 miles.

STRATEGIC FORCES Long-range nuclear missiles that enable the United States and the Soviet Union to attack each other's territory directly. Strategic missiles — which were the subject of the Strategic Arms Limitation Talks (SALT) I and II — include Soviet and U.S. submarine-launched ballistic missiles and bombers as well as intercontinental ballistic missiles such as the MX or the Soviet SS-18. Currently, strategic missiles are the focus of separate talks in Geneva and are excluded from the Euromissile negotiations.

Soviet Union, the United States also proposes the right to short-notice visits to any public or private site that either side suspects may be used to circumvent the agreement. The Soviets are not the only ones to say this may be taking verification too far.

U.S. negotiators were not able to include these proposals for verification arrangements in the draft proposal they took to Geneva in early March. It took another week before the Americans could persuade the five European allies to go along with their verification demands. Although they finally agreed, the five European nations, which balk at the prospect of allowing Soviet inspectors on their military bases, continue to favor less intrusive verification measures.

Despite frictions within the NATO alliance, however, it seemed unlikely after Shultz' Moscow trip that Western Europe would stand in the way of Reagan's first nuclear arms control agreement. Shultz called the Soviet short-range missile offer "a great opportunity for the alliance," though he conditioned its acceptance on consultations with America's NATO allies. Following his consultations with them in Brussels, the foreign ministers of Britain, West Germany and Italy all expressed positive opinions of the Soviet offer, although they deferred official endorsement to the completion of consultations, a process that is expected to take about three weeks.

NATO's Uncertain Posture

The fear of nuclear nakedness has fostered the emergence of a common position on nuclear defense by Britain, West Germany and France. United in the concern that Reagan might enter into an unwise agreement with his Soviet counterpart, the three biggest Western European powers have forged a stronger European pillar of NATO. Sometimes it appears less a component of the Western side than a third party to negotiations between the superpowers.

Britain's emergence as enunciator of the European position on medium-range missiles underlines this trend. Long characterized as Reagan's best friend in Europe, Thatcher has been accused by her opponents — for example, in her defense of the U.S. military attack on Libya last April — of being "Reagan's lap dog." But Britain's special relationship with the United States, based on the two countries' historical and cultural ties, has not prevented it from leading Europe's more independent stance on nuclear defense policy.

Britain maintains an independent nuclear force comprising 64 U.S.-made Polaris submarine-launched ballistic missiles, which the Thatcher government plans to replace with the same number of more modern Trident II missiles beginning early in the 1990s. Both of these long-range missiles are capable of striking targets in the Soviet Union, and Thatcher has made it clear Britain would not want to give up this force. "It is vital that we continue to have an independent nuclear force," she told Reagan during their meeting last year at Camp David.

British and French Independent Arsenals

However, anti-nuclear sentiment, focused on the basing of U.S. F-111s and submarines, both capable of carrying nuclear weapons, grew during the deployment of cruise missiles in Britain beginning in 1983. It has strengthened more recently during the Labor Party's challenge to Thatcher's leadership over the Trident modernization program. Labor leader Neil Kinnock, who may face Thatcher in elections expected to be held this year, has pledged to rid Britain of both its nuclear forces and U.S. forces deployed there as part of NATO's nuclear defense.

France, the only other Western European country with an independent nuclear force, has played an ambivalent role in the Western alliance ever since President Charles de Gaulle withdrew his country from NATO's integrated military command in 1966. Unlike the other European members of NATO, France hosts no allied military forces or military headquarters. Its defense posture has depended increasingly on its nuclear arsenal, which comprises land-based missiles and air-launched weapons as well as submarine-based missiles, all of which can strike targets in the Soviet Union. Unlike Britain, France has built its nuclear deterrent relatively independently, and plans to strengthen it under a modernization plan now under way.

Although Moscow has dropped its insistence that Euromissile limits apply to the nuclear forces of Britain and France, both countries fear that their arsenals may be considered as bargaining chips in future U.S.-Soviet negotiations. Their interest in preventing such a development has encouraged the forging of a new agreement between the two European nuclear powers. Britain and France in March announced plans to cooperate more closely on defense issues, including arrangements to co-produce conventional weapons. France, in particular, has been divided over the prospects of any Euromissile agreement. Its defense minister, Andre Giraud, warned darkly that agreement to remove the Pershing II and cruise missiles would constitute a "nuclear Munich," an act of appeasement that could pave the way for Soviet aggression in the same way Britain and France acquiesced to Hitler's demands before World War II.

Mitterrand, a Socialist, and Conservative Prime Minister Jacques Chirac recognize France's ultimate dependence on the NATO military structure de Gaulle repudiated two decades ago. Meeting March 31 with Reagan in Washington, just as Thatcher was presenting Britain's position to Gorbachev in Moscow, Chirac reiterated his government's concern that any removal of medium-range missiles take place over a long enough period to ensure that the Warsaw Pact does not maintain its advantage in short-range weapons.

This concern is shared by West Germany, which hosts the largest contingent of NATO troops and conventional weaponry, and would stand to bear the heaviest losses in the initial phase of a conventional attack against NATO. Germany's long-standing support for détente stems largely from its desire to smooth relations with East Germany, from which it was split in the wake of World War II. But German enthusiasm for arms control is tempered by an acute awareness of being a front-line state between the two alliances. Because of its location and vulnerability to the Warsaw Pact's superior numbers in conventional forces, Bonn has insisted that NATO retain a short-range nuclear deterrent.

Some Europeans want the informal cooperation among Europe's NATO allies that has grown in the wake of the Iceland summit to be formalized. Chirac has presented a plan for a European defense charter as part of the Western European Union, a little-known organization within the European Economic Community. Composed of Britain, France, West Germany, Italy, Belgium, the Netherlands and Luxembourg, the group's current role is limited to that of a debating forum.

British Foreign Secretary Sir Geoffrey Howe supported this idea in a March 16 address before the Royal Institute of International Relations in Brussels. Emphasizing that Europeans provide the vast majority of NATO's European-based troops and conventional weapons, he called on Europe to "get its own ideas straight" in order to become "a far more rewarding partner for the United States and far more likely to have its views taken seriously...."

U.S. Budget-Cutters Eye NATO Spending

But strengthening Europe's say in matters of the common defense is a delicate task. European criticism of U.S. nuclear policy has long struck a sour note in some quarters in the United States, where the European allies are accused of free-loading at America's expense. While the United States spends 6.7 percent of its gross national product on defense, NATO's European members spend on average less than 4 percent.

One Way to Make a Short-Range Missile

Gen. Maxwell R. Thurman, Army vice chief of staff, suggested in congressional testimony on March 12* that if a Euromissile agreement permitted the West to build up its short-range missile force to match the Soviet force, as was being discussed, then the United States might convert some of its long-range missiles in West Germany into short-range missiles as a cost-effective way to produce short-range missiles. The 1,120-mile-range Pershing II, he said, could be converted into a 460-mile Pershing IB simply by removing a stage from the missile's rocket.

Although Reagan administration officials said the United States had no intention to deploy short-range weapons in Europe, but only wanted to include the right to do so under a Euromissile pact, Thurman's comments sparked a vehement reaction in Moscow. If it is so simple to convert a Pershing II into the shorter-range Pershing IB, it was pointed out, how hard can it be to turn the missile back into a weapon capable of hitting Soviet targets? Indeed, Viktor Karpov, the chief Soviet arms negotiator, called U.S. support for a Euromissile agreement a "bluff," and said the conversion idea proved Washington's bad faith at the negotiating table. Some U.S. observers agreed.

James P. Rubin, assistant director for research for the Arms Control Association, called the conversion issue "an absurdity." He said proposals had been advanced to convert U.S. medium-range missiles into short-range weapons. Ground-launched cruise missiles are very similar to submarine-launched cruise missiles, and could easily be redeployed aboard U.S. submarines. Conversion, Rubin said, "makes a mockery of eliminating a class of weapons, which is how the . . . [medium-range] program has been sold to the public."

*He testified before the Senate Armed Services Conventional Forces Subcommittee.

A large part of U.S. defense expenditures go to Europe, where 330,000 U.S. military personnel are stationed as part of the allied NATO force. Members of Congress who are eager to find ways to cut the growing federal budget deficit are looking more boldly at defense authorizations, which have grown from $180 billion in fiscal 1981, when Reagan came to office, to $290 billion in fiscal 1987. The administration has requested $312 billion for the next fiscal year, which begins Oct. 1.

In their search for ways to cut defense spending, members of Congress are finding U.S. troop presence in Europe a tempting target, especially as the trade deficit with Western European countries continues to grow. "We spend about $150 billion in defense now going to our overseas commitments, and more is in store as the dollar falls in value," Rep. Patricia Schroeder, D-Colo., told reporters on April 6. "Our allies must know that the party is over," she said. "They can do more." Schroeder supports bringing about 200,000 U.S. troops home from Europe over five years. If the Europeans want them to stay, she suggests, the United States should impose a service charge on the countries where they are stationed, equal to the tariffs those countries impose on American imports.

European allies say this argument understates their contribution to NATO. Of the allied forces stationed in Europe in peacetime, Europeans provide most of the military and civilian manpower, as well as "85 percent of the tanks, 95 percent of the artillery and 80 percent of the combat aircraft," according to Dutch Foreign Minister Hans van den Broek.[8] Europeans also emphasize the contributions they make to NATO defense that are less easily calculable than defense expenditures, such as the land where troops and weapons are based and the fact that many NATO members maintain a military draft.

Some American observers also dispute the calls for troop withdrawals from Europe, saying they are not only self-defeating but dangerous. In the view of Richard Burt, the American ambassador to West Germany, "Demobilization of the U.S. forces currently in Europe would leave the United States an army of half a million men. It would turn the U.S. from a superpower into a military and political dwarf." [9]

---

[8] Writing in *Europe*, November 1986, p. 47.
[9] Writing in *The Washington Post*, March 22, 1987.

Recommended Reading List

Books

Blacker, Coit D., *Reluctant Warriors,* W. H. Freeman and Co., 1987.
Garthoff, Raymond L., *Détente and Confrontation,* Brookings Institution, 1985.
Krauss, Melvin, *How NATO Weakens the West,* Simon & Schuster, 1986.
McNamara, Robert S., *Blundering Into Disaster: Surviving the First Century of the Nuclear Age,* Pantheon Books, 1986.
Scribner, Richard A., Theodore J. Ralston and William D. Metz, *The Verification Challenge,* American Association for the Advancement of Science, Birkhäuser, 1985.
Talbott, Strobe, *Deadly Gambits,* Alfred A. Knopf, 1984.

Articles

"A World Without Nuclear Weapons?" *The New York Times Magazine,* April 5, 1987, pp. 45-54, 65.
Schlesinger, James, "Reykjavik and Revelations: A Turn of the Tide?" *Foreign Affairs,* No. 3, 1987.
Schmidt, Helmut, "Defense: A European Viewpoint," *Europe,* November 1986, pp. 13-15, 45.

Reports and Studies

Central Intelligence Agency and Defense Intelligence Agency, "Gorbachev's Modernization Program: A Status Report," March 19, 1987.
Editorial Research Reports: "Science Wars Over Star Wars," 1986 Vol. II, p. 685; "Arms Control Negotiations," 1985 Vol. I, p. 145; "West German 'Missile Election,' " 1983 Vol. I, p. 149.

INDUSTRIAL

COMPETITIVENESS

by

Sarah Glazer

**Mar. 20
1 9 8 7**

America's Global Slippage

A few years ago, it would have seemed unlikely that those fiercely competitive makers of tiny computer chips from Silicon Valley would be banding together to save their industry from Japanese domination. These entrepreneurs, whose minuscule chips were giving us everything from hand calculators to cars that could calculate fuel mileage, seemed the perfect American success story. The clean, high-technology plants in sunny California presented a modern alternative to the grimy steel mills that were closing down in the face of cheap Asian steel.

Yet in March 1986, the nation's computer chip manufacturers decided that they would have to pool their resources and appeal for government funds if they were to match Japan's production techniques. After commanding 80 percent of the world market in 1975, the Americans had slipped to less than 50 percent in 1986 and had conceded first place to the Japanese. As for the high-volume, U.S.-invented "memory chips," which store a computer's information, the American share of the world market had fallen from 100 percent to less than 5 percent in a decade.

Ironically, to save itself, an industry that started out in a typically American way, by inventing a product nobody else had, is now looking at a typically Japanese approach — an industry-government partnership focused on manufacturing quality.

The semiconductor industry's problems with foreign competition have come to the forefront at a time when competitiveness is the political buzzword of the hour. President Reagan proposed a "competitiveness" initiative in his State of the Union speech in January in response, he said, to the charge that "America is losing her competitive edge."

In Congress, where a new caucus on competitiveness was formed this year, the House and Senate are considering "competitiveness" measures to strengthen U.S. retaliation against unfair trading practices by major trading partners. Interest groups ranging from education lobbies to labor unions and business organizations are promoting long-favored legislative solutions or regulatory changes in the name of competitiveness.

Semiconductors: A Problem in Microcosm

In the semiconductor industry, as in industries across the country, companies are not only looking for government help. They also are trying to understand where their manufacturing techniques are inferior to foreign competition.

The new industry consortium — known as Sematech, for Semiconductor Manufacturing Technology Initiative — hopes to build a prototype plant to develop advanced manufacturing techniques and equipment, to be shared by the member companies. The cost of the project — as much as $400 million — is too great an investment for any one of the small companies that typify this industry. The consortium sees the Defense Department as a possible source of funding.

A Pentagon advisory panel, the Defense Science Board, recently recommended that the Pentagon spend $250 million annually to advance the art of semiconductor manufacturing. The panel argued that microelectronics, which are used in missiles and many other weapons, should be domestically produced to protect national security. The national security objections of Pentagon officials earlier this month forestalled the industry-opposed takeover plans of a Japanese company, Fujitsu Ltd., to purchase Fairchild Semiconductor Corp., a major military chip supplier and one of the early Silicon Valley enterprises.

The semiconductor industry's emphasis on the production process mirrors a conclusion increasingly expressed in the business world: that America has paid insufficient attention to the details of manufacturing. Industry executives are concluding that much of the fault for the nation's current loss in trade leadership lies in the way American industry works and in how our society prepares its citizens for the work world. As the United States looks over its shoulder at its main trade rivals — Japan and West Germany — consensus is building that the high-profit mentality of American business executives and financiers is shortsighted and must be changed, and that there must be cooperation between management and labor and improvements in the education and training of American workers.

In the case of semiconductors, Japanese firms look toward the long-term horizon by investing a larger part of their sales in plant, equipment, and research and development than U.S. firms.[1] To develop basic technology, Japanese companies often engage in cooperative arrangements under the aegis of the government's Ministry of International ade and Industry (MITI), which guides industrial growth to maximize the competitiveness of Japanese companies. Cooperation among U.S. firms is restricted by antitrust laws. Sematech spokesmen have conceded, for example, that their plans for the consortium may violate antitrust laws.

Japanese companies accept a lower rate of profitability than that required for a U.S. company to survive, according to the

---

[1] "Report of Defense Science Board Task Force on Defense Semiconductor Dependency," February 1987, Office of the Under Secretary of Defense for Acquisition.

Defense Science Board. The panel attributes this difference to the fact that Japanese companies can borrow money at lower rates than their American competitors. As a general matter, Japanese banks are willing to take greater risks in lending to industrial ventures than are American lenders. In the semiconductor industry, Japanese manufacturers have another advantage. They tend to be part of large, diversified corporations, which can buy as much as 20 percent of their microchip production. American semiconductor manufacturers are frequently small, new companies, which must show a hefty profit quickly to compete for capital in money markets.

Postmortems on U.S. Productivity Lapses

Manufacturing productivity in America has been growing more slowly than in the other leading industrial nations over the past two decades, and now trails Japanese and West German productivity in absolute terms. The comparatively poor U.S. growth rate overshadows the optimism expressed by some economists, such as those on President Reagan's Council of Economic Advisers, that American manufacturing remains healthy because it is now experiencing its highest rate of productivity growth since World War II.

Japan is now the most productive manufacturer in key exporting industries once dominated by the United States — steel, autos, and consumer electronics. Those industries, which provided some of the most lucrative U.S. manufacturing jobs, have suffered continuing employment losses to Europe, Japan and other Asian nations. In the past two decades, America has slipped from the world's No. 1 exporter to No. 3, behind Japan and West Germany. America's slide is sometimes explained in terms of postwar complacency. The United States was the only nation with undamaged factories after World War II, giving it a dominant advantage over potential rivals for at least 15 years. Indeed, in 1960 it was still the world leader. But critics say that American executives took this advantage for granted.

"In an economy where you succeeded almost no matter what you did, management confused its success with its ability to manage," writes Robert Cole, a University of Michigan professor of sociology and business administration who has been researching Japanese work organization for the past 10 years.[2]

The managers of American industry now find themselves on the defensive as the nation questions the reason for its competitive problems. They are starting to re-examine their way of doing things. The senior officers of 180 major manufacturers, in survey results reported by the National Association of Manufac-

[2] See Robert Cole, "What Was Deming's Real Influence?" *Across the Board,* published by the Conference Board, February 1987, pp. 49-51.

turers in February, said they believe roughly half of the improvements in international competitiveness will have to come from changes in corporate policies and practices.

"Essentially we've lost it on the shop floor; we've been beaten in production," concludes Stephen S. Cohen, an economist who directs the Berkeley Roundtable on the International Economy, a research group at the University of California at Berkeley.

Japan's Example: Learning Quality Control

Americans, once the masters of mass production in everything from Fords to cornflakes, have today been surpassed by the Japanese in the science of manufacturing, the critics of industry charge. They contend that from the postwar period through the 1970s, high-level American business managers did not pay attention to the details of production because it was an area of low prestige and low pay. The top business school graduates instead entered marketing and finance. The best engineers went into the development of new products, not into the less-exciting work of manufacturing them.

"Quantity not quality became the norm of postwar American management," writes Cole. Consumer demand was great and managers believed that improved quality meant increased costs.

On the other side of the Pacific Ocean, Japan — a nation devastated by war — was able to shed a reputation for producing shoddy goods by emphasizing quality improvement. Ironically, the chief mentor to the Japanese was an American statistician and quality-control expert named W. Edwards Deming, who was without recognition in the United States.

"With the possible exception of Douglas MacArthur he was the most famous and most revered American in Japan during the postwar years," writes David Halberstam in his new book, *The Reckoning,* about the competition between U.S. and Japanese automakers. Since 1951, the Japanese have annually awarded a medal named for Deming to companies reaching the highest level of quality.

Deming's influence has now come home to America. For example, it was in Japan that Deming promoted the idea of the "quality circle," a small group of employees responsible for ensuring quality in a cooperatively made product. The concept has since been adopted by American companies like Dana Corp., an auto parts supplier based in Toledo, Ohio. "I guess we all had sunglasses on after World War II," said Dana's vice president, William Prebe. "Deming was able to sell his entire strategy to the Japanese. Now we're reading Japanese books" to learn about his work.

According to Cole, Deming drew some of his ideas from the Japanese workplace. The Japanese had developed a participatory system of management that involved all employees and all departments. They also developed a set of checking practices to ensure that the customer's voice was heard throughout the design and production process. As an example of how the Japanese participatory management style can increase productivity, U.S. labor and industry representatives point to the joint venture auto plant owned by General Motors Corp. and Toyota Motor Co. in California. The plant, which produces the Chevrolet Nova, is one of GM's least automated plants but has attained productivity levels on a par with Japanese plants.

The approach to quality advocated by Deming and adopted by the Japanese involves a basic psychological commitment by workers and management to producing the best rather than relying on an outside quality "checker." Writes Halberstam: "One of Deming's American disciples, Ron Moen, said it was as if Deming saw work as a kind of Zen experience. What he is really asking, Moen pointed out, is 'What is the purpose of life, and what is the purpose of work? Why are you doing this? Who truly benefits from what you do other than yourself?' "

In a variation from Japanese culture, Americans have sometimes attached financial incentives when employing quality cir-

191

cles. Nucor Corp., a Charlotte, N.C., company that produces steel products from iron scrap, uses a production incentive system for its non-union workers. The work force is divided into groups of 25-30 people, who are assigned minimum standards of quantity and quality to achieve during the week. If the standards are exceeded, the individual employee receives a weekly bonus pegged to the improvement over the standard.

The average Nucor worker earns about half of his $30,000 wages from these production bonuses, resulting in total pay that is slightly higher than the $28,000 nationwide average for a steelworker, according to Nucor Chairman F. Kenneth Iverson. He says the productivity of his small "mini-mills" is almost triple that of the average U.S. steel mill, which he attributes to the bonus system and to the state-of-the art technology employed by the company.

Management-labor cooperation is seen as a major factor in West Germany's industrial success. In contrast to Japan, however, where labor unions are essentially powerless, West German unions play an important and politically sanctioned role within the industry. In another effort by American managers to improve U.S. industrial competitiveness, some companies are looking toward increased worker-management cooperation as an alternative to the widespread practice of relocating abroad in search of low-paid labor.

General Electric Co. announced in February that it will produce color television receivers at home. The decision was based on an agreement between labor and management to develop improved work practices at its Bloomington, Ind., plant. The leadership of GE and the union — the International Brotherhood of Electrical Workers — "reached an understanding to work together to make the plant more cost-effective to compete against Korean and Japanese companies," said GE spokesman Frank McCann. "That's a bit innovative: both sides have to work together. Otherwise we would have given the business to the Koreans."

Under the agreement, GE will invest $20 million to modernize the plant. Work changes under discussion include easing the job classification system — which limits workers to relatively narrow tasks — and halving the number of work breaks, according to Bill Hacker, business manager for the union's Local 1424.

Are cooperative work agreements the wave of the future? At the United Automobile, Aerospace and Agricultural Implements Workers Union, economist Stephen Beckman said that American workers have had a longstanding interest in participation, but that management has been reluctant to give employees a voice in crucial management decisions, such as the prices of new cars. The auto workers' union will experiment with increased management participation in its agreement with GM for the production of the new Saturn car, slated for production in the mid-1990s. The Saturn program has been described as GM's most intense, high-technology effort to compete with Japanese cars. Under the agreement, GM management is to share decision making at every level with the union, Beckmann said. In exchange, workers will accept up to 20 percent of their pay in production incentives.

The Impact of Technology

Technology is another important factor in America's competitiveness problems. The fact that technological innovations spread so quickly today throughout the world has taken away some of the advantage once enjoyed by an American company with a new product. The ability to copy American products overseas has lent the greatest competitive advantage to those that perfect the manufacture of those products.

Economist Lester C. Thurow of the Massachusetts Institute of Technology points out that "profit margins were once thought to be higher on new, unique products than old, competitive ones. While this may have been true in the past, it is now clear that with foreign competition, higher profit margins on new products do not last anywhere near as long as they used to. ...[T]he long-term profits go to those with the lowest production costs, not to those who make the original discovery." [3]

The semiconductor industry, one of America's leading export industries, learned Thurow's economic lesson the hard way. In 1971, only American firms sold the first memory chips, known as 1K, for the 1,000 bits of memory they could hold. Two years later, only American firms produced chips with higher, 4K memory, capacity, and Japanese firms were shipping less than 10 percent of the 1K chips made worldwide.

As the race heated up and the memory capacity of new chips increased, American and Japanese firms were neck and neck in introducing 64K chips in the early 1980s. Today, American firms fear that the Japanese will surpass them in the quality, volume and capacity of memory chips. The Japanese success secret once again is quality in the manufacturing process, especially applicable for tiny microchips, which require fine tolerances in manufacturing.

[3] See Lester C. Thurow, "American Industrial Competition," *Current*, December 1985, pp. 23-29.

Share of
World Manufacturing Exports

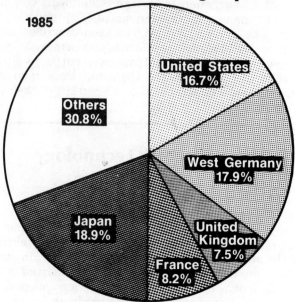

1985

United States
16.7%

Others
30.8%

West Germany
17.9%

Japan
18.9%

United Kingdom
7.5%

France
8.2%

Exports of 14 major industrial countries.
Source: Commerce Department

In consumer electronics, too, American firms now have few unique competitive advantages. Before 1960, most of the significant technical advances in television came from the United States. Today, the manufacturing techniques for televisions are well-known and are the same the world over. Low-wage operations in Taiwan and South Korea, for example, have increasingly replaced American factories. Half the U.S. consumer electronics market has been taken by imports, and most products assembled in the United States contain many imported components.[4]

The Japanese currently build about 95 percent of the world's videocassette recorders for home use, although an American company — Ampex Corp. — pioneered video recording on magnetic tape for broadcast applications.[5] The Japanese reaped their advantage by investing years of effort in the manufacture of a consumer equivalent, says John Alic, an analyst at the congressional Office of Technology Assessment.

In some instances, however, high technology may offer American managers an avenue for a comeback. Even in industries threatened with low-wage competition in Asian countries, uses

[4] John A. Alic and Martha Caldwell Harris, "Employment lessons from the electronics industry," *Monthly Labor Review,* February 1986.
[5] Office of Technology Assessment, *International Competitiveness in Electronics,* November 1983.

of new technology are carving out areas for American and European survivors. In the apparel industry, where "Made in Singapore" labels abound, some American and European companies are relying on computerized sales information and flexible production to maximize efficiency. Benetton Inc., a fast-growing Italian manufacturer of casual clothes with 600 retail outlets around the world, reaped net profits of 10.2 percent and sales of $831 million last year despite its reliance on high-wage Italian workers.

"Every time a kid in Washington, D.C., buys a Benetton sweater, a microchip transmits the sale back to Italy," said Cohen of the Berkeley research group, thus providing instant inventory control and the ability to order and change production in response to sales. A Benetton spokeswoman explained that the company views a sale as an order, and "We don't make things until they're ordered." As a result, the company doesn't have to carry costly, unsold inventory.

High School Basics Favor the Japanese

Educational differences between the United States and Japan are frequently cited as a reason that the American work force is becoming less competitive. The Japanese place much greater emphasis on secondary education than on higher education. In Japan, where the high school graduation rate is 90 percent, compared with 80 percent in the United States, a high school graduate is better prepared for the technical work world than an American. In Japan, large numbers of students who do not go to college get technical, vocational or semiprofessional schooling as preparation for jobs in industry. The result is a large pool of

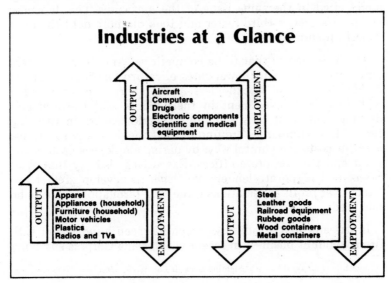

Industries at a Glance

OUTPUT

EMPLOYMENT

Aircraft
Computers
Drugs
Electronic components
Scientific and medical
equipment

OUTPUT

EMPLOYMENT

Apparel
Appliances (household)
Furniture (household)
Motor vehicles
Plastics
Radios and TVs

OUTPUT

EMPLOYMENT

Steel
Leather goods
Railroad equipment
Rubber goods
Wood containers
Metal containers

well-prepared candidates for "gray-collar" technical jobs. Japanese industry also stresses on-the-job training. By contrast, the American system does a poor job of preparing students who do not go on to college. Even among high school graduates, functional illiteracy is common, according to the Office of Technology Assessment.

Of course, some American advantages are not exhibited in the statistics. Japanese education tends to emphasize learning by rote, while the American system is aimed at encouraging debate and inventiveness. That different philosophy, many say, shows up in American industry, where the main interest has always been in inventing something new, not in producing someone else's invention.

Strategies for Competition

A merican business managers have been criticized for taking a short-term view of company profits. Surveys of business executives cited in *Business Week* magazine in 1985 indicate that Japanese executives are most interested in making their companies global leaders while American managers place most emphasis on increasing the value of their company's shares.[6] In the chemical and electronics industries, Japanese companies on average turned in after-tax profits that were only about half those of their American counterparts, according to another study cited in the same issue of the magazine. The Japanese companies grew a third faster and took on more debt than the American companies.

All this suggests that to be competitive, American managers may have to settle for lower rates of return and less attractive dividends to their stockholders in the short-term — coupled with increased investment in their plants and research and development — if they want to be world leaders in the long term. Many companies are finding that the only way to survive is to cut costs the painful way: by paring employees both in the plant and the corporate offices. Executives also say that Wall Street and corporate lenders will have to develop greater patience over profit expectations if the long-term approach is to be nurtured.

In the auto parts industry, which has seen hundreds of U.S. firms go out of business in recent years, Dana Corp. is surviving

---

[6] Judith H. Dobrzynski et al., "Fighting Back: It Can Work," *Business Week*, Aug. 26, 1985, pp. 62-68.

by turning itself into a much leaner company. While investing in automated equipment and reducing factory and corporate staff, Dana has experienced a significantly lower rate of return than its corporate managers once considered acceptable (less than 10 percent last year, compared with its 15 percent objective). The firm also showed a sizable loss last year when it sold off some unprofitable side businesses.

Nevertheless, its stock has improved dramatically, according to Dana economist Prebe. He takes this as a sign that Wall Street is moving away from American business' "shortsighted" view. The auto market today, he notes, is a mature market, and "we have to take a smaller share of what remains.... You're going to have fewer survivors. Some people won't make it." In this kind of market, Prebe adds, "lower cost is the only way to make profits."

Black & Decker Corp., the power tool manufacturer, adopted a similar strategy when the Japanese competition cut the American firm's share of the world market from 20 percent to 15 percent in 1980.[8] The company reduced its work force by 40 percent, pumped $80 million into plant modernization, adopted Japanese manufacturing concepts at home and began making tools overseas. The firm says it regained its 20 percent market share but had to meet lower Japanese prices, eroding its profits.

Linking Bank Lending to Business Needs

A major reason American business cites for taking a short-term outlook is the higher cost of capital in this country than in Japan. A 1983 report by the Office of Technology Assessment, for example, found a 5 percent capital cost difference in the electronics industry.[9] The major reasons for the lower cost of capital in Japan, the report said, are Japanese government subsidies, the close relationship between Japanese industry and banks, and Japan's high rate of savings, which tends to lower interest rates for companies seeking to borrow. Household savings in Japan run at about 20 percent of income — nearly four times the rate in the United States. West German savings rates are about twice those in this country.

Banks in Japan accept greater risks in lending capital to industrial firms than would be acceptable in the United States. In America, it is the stockholders who take a gamble on a company's future. They accept a risky stake in the company, and in exchange, their investment — known as equity — commands a higher price than the less risk-oriented banker's debt. Debt is a more conservative form of capital in which creditors,

---

[8] Dobrzynski et al., *op. cit.*, p. 64.
[9] "International Competitiveness in Electronics," Office of Technology Assessment, November 1983.

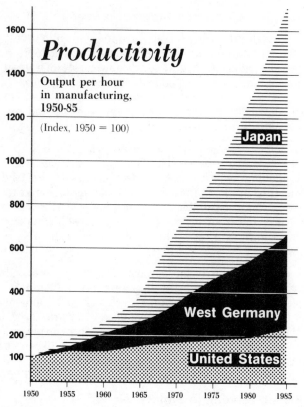

Productivity

Output per hour
in manufacturing,
1950-85

(Index, 1950 = 100)

Japan

West Germany

United States

1950 1955 1960 1965 1970 1975 1980 1985

Source: Bureau of Labor Statistics

such as bondholders or banks, accept a lower rate of interest than stockholders in exchange for first claim on the company's assets if it goes under.

American businesses often point to the high proportions of debt used by the Japanese to finance their companies as a reason that capital is cheaper to the Japanese firm. By U.S. standards, Japanese banks assume quasi-equity positions by accepting so much debt in industrial firms. Along with their larger stake, the banks often are involved in restructuring a troubled business or infusing cash into it if they have lent it capital. It is a role that would be alien to an American bank except in bankruptcies.

Banks in West Germany are even more closely tied to business than in Japan. German banks are allowed to hold unrestricted amounts of common stock in manufacturing companies. Three German banks have seats on the boards of 70 of the 100 largest German corporations. German business, like Japan's, has higher debt-to-equity ratios than is common in the United States.[10]

---

[10] *Ibid.*

Industrial Competitiveness

Since World War II, Japan has used commercial banks to guide its decisions about government policy. They have extended credit, for example, to industry at the expense of consumer credit. At the same time, government influence over the lending decisions of major banks in Japan is considerably greater than in almost any Western nation, including the United States and West Germany. The government holds a majority ownership in the central bank, the Bank of Japan. In the past, Japan favored "target" industries with low-cost capital, but recent studies say this practice is no longer as prevalent. Nevertheless, continuing working relationships among government, industry and banks may make it possible to continue favoring certain industries in an informal way.

U.S. executives are urging the government to help them fight the powerful government-industry-banking triads operating in Japan and Europe. "As soon as possible," urged the National Association of Manufacturers in February, "the government should ... offer American companies the financing support they need to make them competitive with foreign manufacturers that benefit from effective and determined government financing programs."

It is often difficult to find direct evidence that the Japanese government has provided a subsidy to a target industry. Specific Japanese industries or companies may be favored, instead, through a consensus among competing industries under the direction of MITI. Japan specialist Ezra Vogel of Harvard University describes this process in *Ideology and National Competitiveness*: "Many of these strategies simply involve frequent discussions that clarify opportunities.... The Japanese government and quasi-government institutions give far less direct aid than most foreigners imagine, but subsidies and tax incentives are available when a sector needs to be restructured or when important activities that companies could not do themselves need to be made possible."

For example, in the mid-1970s, as markets for manufactured goods became saturated, MITI helped form consortia of Japanese industries to undertake large construction projects and encouraged private insurance firms to provide coverage, reducing the risks of those ventures.[11] When the market for a product is saturated — as in steel, shipbuilding and textiles — cartels are formed to work out formulas for reducing total production. It is common under these circumstances, Vogel said, for the government to subsidize the destruction of a company's outmoded facilities so that only the most modern and competitive facilities will remain.

---

[11] See Ezra F. Vogel, *Japan as Number One*, Harvard University Press, 1979.

Trade-Protectionism Issues

A nother part of the problem, American industry charges, is the collusion of foreign governments with their industries to bar American products from their markets and to invade traditionally American markets with below-cost pricing. As the competitiveness debate unfolds, industry groups will be pushing for legislative changes they think will tilt the competitive scale in their favor. The National Association of Manufacturers foresees an increased role for government and for "creative cooperation" between it and the private sector. "At the least, a more intelligent and supportive government role will be required in many areas, such as technology transfer, regulatory reform, exchange rates and trade policy," the manufacturers' group has said.

The disappointment of American semiconductor manufacturers over the failure of a recent U.S.-Japan trade agreement foreshadows the major political debate over trade legislation. The concern in semiconductors, as in many other industries, surrounds Japan's use of "predatory pricing," a technique made famous when John D. Rockefeller priced his gasoline below cost to drive neighboring stations out of business. Japanese chip makers operate at a loss in order to seize market share from existing competitors, U.S. industry charges.

An American-Japanese trade agreement was negotiated last July to prevent the Japanese from "dumping" their chips in the U.S. market at below fair market value. U.S. negotiators charge that the agreement has been circumvented by Japanese companies, who are dumping their chips in third-country markets for as little as half the production cost in the knowledge that those chips will eventually find their way to the American market. The U.S. industry also charges that the agreement was ineffective in removing Japanese trade barriers to the sale of U.S. chips in Japan.

President Reagan's inability to force Japan's hand on a negotiated basis has spurred Congress to consider requiring the president to retaliate with quotas or other trade barriers against U.S. trade rivals. As Congress takes up the debate, the main issue of controversy will be how to toughen existing trade laws. Last year, the House passed a measure that would have required the president to impose trade barriers against nations that have trade surpluses with the United States. Reagan has vigorously opposed any measure that would require him to retaliate. Current law leaves discretion with the president. Both the National Association of Manufacturers and the Chamber of Commerce of the United States are backing strengthened retaliatory measures, although the Chamber would leave final discretion with the president. Labor unions are backing last year's House-passed measure.

In offering solutions to the problem of competitiveness, certain items appear on almost every list, namely improvements in education and job training for displaced workers. Old proposals have also been revived under the new name of competitiveness. In the case of industry, well-known reruns include eased anti-trust laws, changes in environmental regulations, increased federal spending on research and development and restoration of the recently eliminated investment tax credit.

President Reagan's massive "competitiveness" proposal features a $1 billion job training program, the establishment of new science and technology centers at universities, changes in anti-trust laws, and minor changes in U.S. trade laws. Reagan's proposal also includes numerous changes he has been seeking in other programs, such as repeal of the auto fuel mileage standards, which appear to have little to do with competitiveness.

Smoot-Hawley Tariff: Failed Protectionism

Whether protectionism works is a question that won't likely be resolved any time soon. But when America tried protectionism in 1930, it backfired disastrously. The Smoot-Hawley Act of that year capped a decade of political isolationism. It boosted average tariff rates on imports by nearly 50 percent, affecting hundreds of items. The law was enacted in the hope that it would protect employment. Instead, it led to retaliation by foreign governments and contributed to the length and severity of the Great Depression. In 1934, Congress shifted gears and gave the president the power, in effect, to undo the law by negotiating tariff reductions of as much as 50 percent on specific commodities with individual nations.

After World War II, America was the driving force behind an international agreement that moved away from protectionism. Under the 1947 General Agreement on Tariffs and Trade (GATT), the world's major trading partners have negotiated seven rounds of tariff reduction. Protectionist moves are still possible, however, under an "escape clause" in the pact. This permits a country to opt out of negotiated tariff reductions and reinstate trade barriers if increased imports can be shown to cause or threaten serious injury to domestic producers. In the United States, requests for protection are made through the International Trade Commission. It determines whether the industry has been seriously injured and recommends the type of trade relief needed to the president.

Neither Congress nor the president is likely to heed business pleas for government aid in reducing the cost of capital on any grand scale. Taxpayer-backed financing is considered too expensive in view of the large federal budget deficit. Many of the tax breaks sought by business were rejected or repealed by Congress in the Tax Reform Act that went into effect in January.

Job Training and Protectionist Proposals

As Congress and the president debate how to solve the question of competitiveness, an enduring question will be how much the government can contribute. A major element of Reagan's package is a $1 billion job retraining program for workers displaced from dying industries. Although everyone likes the idea of job retraining, past federal programs have a less than glowing record. The Job Training Partnership Act of 1982, initiated in response to a deep economic recession and still in existence, reached no more than 5 percent of eligible workers in its first two years at a cost of up to $900 per worker, the Office of Technology Assessment reported last February.[12]

In coming months, labor, together with some segments of industry, will be urging stronger protectionist measures. In the past decade, the percentage of imports covered by protection has almost tripled in response to individual industries' requests, and more than 22 percent of imports are now covered by quotas, levies or other forms of protection. The increasing pleas for relief are "like a thermometer for measuring the fever" of competition, says Paula Stern, former chairwoman of the International Trade Commission and now senior associate at the Carnegie Endowment for International Peace. At the Chamber of Commerce, chief economist Richard Rahn argues that protectionism in the end hurts the country that uses it. He points to the $10-a-pound price that Japanese housewives pay for beef and high prices for other U.S. food products burdened with tariffs and other trade restrictions.

But labor economist Beckman at the auto workers' union disagrees, arguing that protectionism is necessary for a country to survive. "Every country is deciding what they're going to produce in their country," he said. "The U.S. is the only country that doesn't have a strategy. . . . The U.S. is not going to become competitive by engaging in commercial competition with state-supported competitors."

Jobs are the essential requirement for a strong economy, Beckman emphasizes, because people buy products with in-

---

[12] "Technology and Structural Unemployment: Reemploying Displaced Adults," Office of Technology Assessment, February 1986.

come, further fueling the economy. The claims that the U.S. economy is doing fine, Beckman argues, do not take into account American industry's reliance on cheap overseas labor for its own products. About 19 percent of the goods imported to this country come from U.S.-affiliated companies, according to the Office of Technology Assessment staff.

In the end, no matter what policy Americans employ, they will discover that they live in an ever-shrinking world. Insulation cannot be provided by protectionist measures, Stern warns: "You don't know whether you're competitive unless you measure yourself against others. . . . If you close off the imports, you'll for sure not become competitive. You won't need to."

Once the United States stood like a colossus over the postwar world, magnanimously promoting free trade. Today, America is faced with those once small nations challenging it eye to eye. The competitiveness debate is a sign that all sides in this country have recognized a major historical change: the United States is now more like other nations, forced to compete.

Recommended Reading List

Books

Halberstam, David, *The Reckoning,* William Morrow, 1986.
Lodge, George C., and Ezra F. Vogel, eds., *Ideology and National Competitiveness: An Analysis of Nine Countries,* Harvard, 1987.
Vogel, Ezra F., *Japan as Number One: Lessons for America,* Harvard, 1979.

Articles

Kutscher, Ronald E., and Valerie Personick, "Deindustrialization and the Shift to Services," *Monthly Labor Review,* June 1986.
Thurow, Lester C., "American Industrial Competition: A World Class Economy," *Current,* December 1985.

Reports and Studies

Committee for Economic Development, "Work and Change: Labor Market Adjustment in a Competitive World," December 1986.
Defense Science Board Task Force, "Defense Semiconductor Dependency," February 1987, Office of the Under Secretary of Defense for Acquisition, Department of Defense.
Editorial Research Reports: "Textiles: Push for Protectionism," 1985 Vol. II, p. 757; "Productivity and the New Work Ethic," 1972 Vol. I, p. 291.
President's Commission on Industrial Competitiveness, "Global Competition: The New Reality," January 1985.
Office of Technology Assessment, "International Competitiveness in Electronics," November 1983.

Graphics: P. 185, Goodyear; p. 190, Boeing, Goodyear, New United Motor and Sverdrup Corp.

INDEX